THE REAL READER'S QU

Slightly foxed

'U and I and Me'

NO.79 AUTUMN 2023

Editors: Gail Pirkis & Hazel Wood
Marketing & publicity: Steph Allen, Jennie Harrison Bunning & Hattie Summers
Subscriptions, orders & bookshops: Jess Dalby

Cover illustration: Maxwell Doig, *Southwold Rooftops II*, acrylic on canvas on panel, 86 x 64 cm.
Image courtesy of David Messum Fine Art Ltd

Maxwell Doig was born in Huddersfield and trained at Manchester School of Art. He undertook postgraduate studies at the Slade and at UCL where he also studied anatomy. In 1990 he had his first solo show with the Hart Gallery, Nottingham, and won the Joseph Webb Prize for Draughtsmanship. In the early 1990s, he was Artist in Residence at the Hochschule Der Kunst, Berlin. Returning to Huddersfield, he set up his first studio at Slaithwaite and started to explore aerial compositions. He won the Villiers David Prize in 1997 and then travelled throughout the USA, as well Australia and Mexico. He is represented by David Messum Fine Art, London.

Back cover fox by James Nunn
Design by Octavius Murray
Layout by Andrew Evans
Colophon and tailpiece by David Eccles

Published by Slightly Foxed Limited
53 Hoxton Square
London N1 6PB

tel 020 7033 0258
email office@foxedquarterly.com
www.foxedquarterly.com

Slightly Foxed is published quarterly in early March, June, September and December

Annual subscription rates (4 issues)
UK and Ireland £56; Overseas £64

Single copies of this issue can be bought for £14.50 (UK) or £16.50 (Overseas)

All back issues in printed form are also available

ISBN 978-1-910898-85-7

ISSN 1742-5794

Printed and bound by Smith Settle, Yeadon, West Yorkshire

Contents

Contents

Isla Middleton

From the Editors

New contributors to *Slightly Foxed* sometimes ask us which issue their piece is going to appear in and the truth is, we're usually hard put to tell them in advance. One pleasure of *SF* is that we're not bound by publication dates for new books, so we rarely plan a piece for a particular issue but instead welcome good contributions and select from what we have. We've always worked on the bran-tub principle that we'd like readers to dip in and find something un-expected that they wouldn't normally have been looking for. But despite this, each issue does seem to come together with a particular atmosphere and character of its own.

Not unexpectedly, this issue has a somewhat autumnal feel that goes with evenings drawing in, fallen leaves underfoot and a chill in the air. It features, among other things, a hunting memoir, a look into the strange interior world of the neurologist Oliver Sacks, a tale of gothic horror, and memories from the courtiers who waited on Queen Victoria in the draughty drawing-rooms and icy bedrooms at Balmoral, where only the passages were heated. As Prince Albert said to the children's governess Lady Lyttleton when asked one bitterly cold day to check her accounts: 'Yes, certainly, if you will consent to my doing reel steps all the time to warm myself.'

Our latest Slightly Foxed edition also has a distinctly autumnal flavour. Richard Cobb's *A Classical Education* (see p.11), written in his inimitable, minutely observed and quietly menacing style, is more like a psychological thriller than a straightforward memoir. Cobb and his friend Edward were given the 'classical education' of the title at their public school, Shrewsbury, where they became close enough to visit one another's homes in the holidays. After school Richard lost track of Edward – until he read the appalling news that his friend had murdered his mother. Fourteen years later Cobb meets Edward again and looks back with wonder and dismay at the extraordinary events that led up to the murder.

There's also another excellent addition to our Plain Foxed series – SFEs which have sold out in the limited edition but are still very much in demand. *To War with Whitaker* is the entertaining and down-to-earth diary kept by Hermione, Countess of Ranfurly, after she decided to follow her husband Dan to war when he was called up in 1939. Accompanying Dan was their characterful cook-butler Whitaker of the title. However, Yeomanry rules decreed that though officers could take their servants they could not take their wives. Undeterred, Hermione made her own way through the wartime chaos, working for the Special Operations Executive in Cairo, and for General Jumbo Wilson in Jerusalem. It's a unique behind-the-scenes picture of the war in the Middle East and the Mediterranean as seen by a very unconventional aristocrat.

Finally, a reminder that Readers' Day this year is on Saturday, 4 November at the Art Workers' Guild, our home-from-home in Queen Square, London. There'll be the usual selection of excellent speakers, plus the chance to visit our pop-up bookshop and enjoy the pleasure of coffee and chat with other Fox readers, so do book your tickets soon to avoid disappointment.

GAIL PIRKIS & HAZEL WOOD

U and I and Me

GEORGE COCHRANE

I hadn't read much John Updike when I picked up Nicholson Baker's book on him during lockdown; but then neither had Baker when he wrote the book. This is one of the novelties of *U and I*. Where most non-fiction strives for mastery of its subject, this little book pursues that 'very spottiness of coverage [that] is, along with the wildly un-tenable generalizations that spring from it, one of the most important features of the thinking we do about living writers'. The result is a funny, profound meditation on what writers actually mean to readers as opposed to what academics tell us they should mean.

To say that Updike is a 'living writer' does date the book, of course. When *U and I* was published in 1991, however, there was no writer more alive than John Updike. He had just won his second Pulitzer Prize for the final novel in his 'Rabbit' tetralogy, he was still writing oodles of short stories and criticism for the *New Yorker*, and he had eighteen more years of equally absurd productivity ahead of him. Not that Baker could know this last part: indeed it is his very anxieties about his hero's mortality that spur him to write about Updike. 'To wait until a writer has died', he reasons,

> seemed to me . . . to go directly counter to one of the principal
> aims of the novel itself, which is to capture pieces of mental life
> as truly as possible, as they unfold, with all the surrounding
> forces of circumstance . . . The commemorative essay that pops

Nicholson Baker, *U and I: A True Story* (1991)
Granta · Pb · 192pp · £8.99 · ISBN 9781847083517

up in some periodical, full of sad-clown sorrowfulness the year following the novelist's death . . . is unworthy of the fine-tuned descriptive capacities of the practising novelist.

No. If he's going to write about Updike, 'it has to be done while he is alive'.

Having 'almost no idea what I was going to be able to say, only that I did have things to say', Baker begins with some ground rules.

The first is that he cannot read or reread a word more of Updike than he has already read, which, as I've mentioned, is surprisingly little: just eight of Updike's then thirty-odd books in their entirety. To 'supplement or renew my impressions with fresh draughts of Updike' would mean 'a multiplicity of examples would compete to illustrate a single point, in place of the one example that had made the point seem worth making in the first place'.

The second is that any quotation must be done from memory. Only when the book is finished can Baker reopen Updike and check his recall (with the correct quotations put in parentheses after the incorrect).

The results are fascinating. Though Baker's recall is good, it is inevitably imperfect, sometimes wildly misremembering quotes, sometimes inventing them entirely. But accuracy is not the point. The point (which Baker proves beyond doubt) is that memory is always partial, and that to write about writers with all their works to hand is not actually true to how we think about them ninety-nine per cent of the time. We only ever have 'an idea' of a writer, not a full knowledge of them. This is most true of the living writer; their life and work being incomplete, we cannot but have a partial knowledge of them.

And it is when we don't have a full grasp of something, I suggest, that we resent it. Which brings me to one of the main joys of *U and I*: its envy. For as much as Baker admires that 'serious, Prousto-Nabokovian, morally sensitive, National Book Award-winning prose style' of his subject, he also hates him for it. One of his bitterest recollections is of

> an amazing performance by Updike on Dick Cavett . . . where he spoke in swerving, rich, complex paragraphs of unhesitating intelligence that he finally allowed to glide to rest at the curb with a little downward swallowing smile of closure, as if he almost felt that he ought to apologize for his inability even to fake the need to grope for his expression.

Another is of a 1980s documentary on Updike in which its subject talks eloquently to camera while doing some housework: 'I was stunned to recognize that with Updike we were dealing with a man so naturally verbal that he could write his fucking memoirs *on a ladder!*' Clive James was understating it, in my view, when he called this book 'screamingly funny'.

What's funniest about Baker's idea of Updike, though, is the sense he has of him as a friend. If only Updike knew how much they had in common – psoriasis, insomnia, an overly close relationship with their mothers – then they surely would be friends, Baker feels, before deciding that the amount of time he's spent thinking about him makes them friends already. Hence his feelings of 'hurt' when he learns that 'another youngish writer . . . living in the Boston area' has been invited to play golf with Updike, not him; hence his conviction that *he* is the inspiration for the tall, pimply youth in Updike's novel *Roger's Version* (1986). Baker doesn't seem quite so obsessed at the time of writing, thankfully, the book's past tense giving its author an ironic distance from his younger self that is crucial to its comedy: 'It may seem incredible, given how little I had published and how bad it was, that I could have even idly theorized as to why Updike wasn't making an effort to seek me out, but I did.' Were he still theorizing such things, the book would just have been creepy.

As it is, *U and I* has given me as much pleasure on the second reading as it did on my first three years ago. Of course, if I *really* admired the book, I should probably have kept it closed and written this piece from memory, but then that would have been to deny myself the delights of Baker's prose, which, despite its author's inferiority complex, is just as baroque and brilliant as Updike's. It would also have denied me some much-needed solidarity. For in the years since Baker first impressed on me the genius of John Updike, I too have seen the light and become something of an Updike obsessive myself; practically every other book I read has his name on it. And that's a lonely thing to be when you're 25 years old and Updike is as out of fashion as he currently is. What I've been in need of is a friend who understands; understands what it's like to be addicted to a writer so prolific that there is an almost limitless supply of him. In Nicholson Baker I think I've found that friend.

GEORGE COCHRANE is a writer and editor from remotest Northumberland. He now lives and works in London, where the air isn't quite so clear.

An Unusual Case

MARTIN SORRELL

Richard Cobb's memoir *A Classical Education* (1985) opens on a spring day in 1950. He is at St Lazare station in Paris awaiting the arrival of an old schoolfriend he's not seen for fourteen years. Cobb has spent much of that time on the Continent, first as a soldier in the war and then as a historian researching various French archives. His friend, by contrast, has been shut away in a Dublin asylum for the entirety of those years, serving out his sentence for the murder of his mother.

The boat train arrives and empties, and there's Cobb's friend striding along the platform. Apart from the weight he's put on, it's the same tall, curly-haired Edward – the surname is withheld from us, tactfully in the circumstances – who had shown newly arrived Richard the ropes at Shrewsbury School. Almost his first words after so long take Cobb by surprise: 'What a pity that we went to a classical school.' That expression of regret is the one explicit connection between the title of the book and its contents. Edward's regret is that their type of school didn't have weapons-cleaning on the syllabus. If only it had, he'd have known that to rid his axe entirely of blood, he should have washed it in cold water, not hot. That, Edward tells Cobb in all seriousness, is where Shrewsbury failed in the duty it owed him personally.

Cobb is dismayed that matricide and lengthy incarceration appear to have wrought no change in his friend, who's as unburdened by self-awareness as he was fourteen years earlier, and who shows no sign of remorse or guilt for what has happened. Even now he's fully an adult, he remains incomplete, an innocent at large, convinced he'd have got away with murder if only his school had taught him the things that mattered.

*

Edward had already been at Shrewsbury for a year when Cobb arrived and was allocated to his house, Rigg's. The two hit it off immediately, bonding over a shared love of pranks and practical jokes (one of which, played on a particularly oleaginous chaplain, Cobb describes with relish). The boys' backgrounds were very different; Richard's in Tunbridge Wells, a model of middle-class decorum, Edward's in Dublin, one hundred per cent dysfunctional, as Richard would see for himself when he spent a few days one summer with Edward and his mother in her house – 'home' decidedly not the word – in Booterstown. Edward had warned Richard beforehand about his estranged parents, monsters he could bring himself to call only Moloch and Medea. The two were locked in a war-without-end, with Edward the collateral damage.

Moloch had all but washed his hands of Edward, but not so Medea, hell-bent on destroying her son. Richard had to watch as a row between mother and son progressed from words to weapons. Initially, Edward was no match for the fourteen-stone, alcohol-soaked wrecking-ball that was Medea. He remained silent and still, impotent with rage. But when she aimed a full teapot at his head, narrowly missing it, he walked off, boiled a kettle, made a fresh cup of tea, came back and threw it in his mother's face (effects not recorded). A pitched artillery battle followed, fought with whatever objects came to hand until ammunition ran out and hostilities ceased, to be resumed no doubt at the next opportunity.

Medea had it in for Richard too, though in his case she limited her attacks to words. Accusing him of leading her boy astray, she sent him packing back to England well before the agreed date. Matters didn't stop there. She then tried to sue Richard for the 'libels' about her which she'd found in some jokey letters he'd written to Edward. That failed. So a few months later, she wrote – in green ink, Cobb notes with disgust – to every male college in Oxford and Cambridge to warn them against scholarship candidate Cobb. That too failed, and in the autumn of 1935, Cobb started at Merton College, Oxford.

By then he and Edward had gone their separate ways and Cobb assumed he'd hear nothing more of Medea. But in February 1936, splashed across the newspapers, came the news that she'd been hacked to death and that Edward was to stand trial for her murder. Since it was likely that Cobb would be subpoenaed as a prosecution witness, the Oxford CID advised him to spend the coming vacation in Brussels and not Paris as he'd intended; unlike France, Belgium didn't have an extradition treaty with the Irish Free State. The trial went ahead without Cobb, Edward was carted off to Dundrum Asylum and the two didn't meet again until the reunion at St Lazare station.

*

A Classical Education is not an easy book to classify. The title suggests a chronologically arranged memoir of schooldays; or perhaps an essay on pedagogy, the ancients versus the moderns, art versus science, and so on. But it's neither. Most obviously it's a psychological thriller, fluently developed. It makes no odds that the denouement is known from the start. A dramatist might have shaped the events into a tragedy for our times. But Cobb is no tragedian. His forte is the rattling good story. And, as he concedes in his preface, where the passage of time has created gaps in memory, fictions have filled them in.

A rattling good story *A Classical Education* certainly is, one that Cobb often dined out on in Oxford when he returned in the 1960s as a don. But of course it *is* a memoir too, the biography of a friendship between two lads drawn together by their similarities but ultimately separated by the sad reality that while one of them has grown up, the other has not and probably cannot. Initially, I wondered if the book's title was meant ironically. Education? What education? Then I thought no, irony wasn't really Cobb's way. But now I'm changing my mind again. Shrewsbury may have set Cobb on his zigzag path to honours and distinction; but Edward, unchanging, incorrigible Edward? *His* classical education appears to have taught him nothing worthwhile, not even how to out damned spots from an axe.

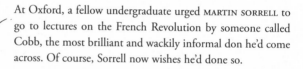

At Oxford, a fellow undergraduate urged MARTIN SORRELL to go to lectures on the French Revolution by someone called Cobb, the most brilliant and wackily informal don he'd come across. Of course, Sorrell now wishes he'd done so.

Richard Cobb's *A Classical Education* (192pp) is now available in a limited and numbered cloth-bound edition of 2,000 copies (subscribers: UK & Ireland £18, Overseas £20; non-subscribers: UK & Ireland £20, Overseas £22). All prices include post and packing. Copies may be ordered by post (53 Hoxton Square, London N1 6PB), by phone (020 7033 0258) or via our website www.foxedquarterly.

Such Devoted Sisters

KATE YOUNG

I read Shirley Jackson's *We Have Always Lived in the Castle* (1962) one summer as a teenager. It's a work of gothic horror, and a mystery novel. More specifically, it's a strange, haunting story about a town that fears and is obsessed by two of its residents following the fatal poisoning of their family. I have always thought of it as a book about sisters, about Merricat and Constance, 'two halves of the same person'. Endlessly self-absorbed, I spent my first reading thinking of my own sister. Our relationship was the most important and the most constant in my life, as we moved back and forth between the homes of our divorced parents. And so, of course, in the heat of the summer, with my sister my main source of company, I felt that this book had been written specifically for me.

I took it entirely literally, considering the world it presented as though it could reasonably become my own. Would I act as Constance did should *my* younger, more tempestuous sister murder our family by adding arsenic to the sugar bowl before dessert? Would I carry the blame on my shoulders; would I hope for and rely on the same insufficient evidence that resulted in Constance's acquittal? Would I, for my sister's sake, sit politely through tea and cake with the gossiping neighbours who thought it was me who had murdered my family? Would I, like Constance, fill the house with things my sister loved to eat – with jars of pickled rhubarb, with eggs, done 'soft and buttery', with roast lamb and mint, with tiny, sweet carrots and spring salads?

Shirley Jackson, *We Have Always Lived in the Castle* (1962)
Penguin · Pb · 176pp · £9.99 · ISBN 9780141191454

Would I submit to the prison we built for ourselves, a castle I would never leave? Would I decide that's how I might be happiest?

I would, I knew, even then. All I needed was my sister. For my sister, I would be a Constance.

In fact in Jackson's first drafts Constance and Jenny – as Merricat was originally called – were written as friends, two women who plotted the death of one of their husbands. Jackson's plan was for Jenny to be a character 'absolutely secure in her home and her place in the world, so much so that she can dispose of her husband without concern'. Merricat and Constance are sisters, but *We Have Always Lived in the Castle* is really a story about women, particularly those who exist outside the place that has been marked out for them.

Jackson's books are peopled with women who live on the fringes, women who can't or don't or won't conform. In Ruth Franklin's biography, *A Rather Haunted Life* (2016), she writes of how, from a young age, Jackson herself failed to conform comfortably to the feminine ideal that society, her conservative community and her mother set out for her. As a child, to escape her own loneliness, she wrote stories about lonely people who felt 'different' but she never showed them to anyone. She married Stanley Edgar Hyman, a literary critic and academic, who had multiple affairs throughout their marriage, and lived with him and their four children in North Bennington in Vermont (a town that served as inspiration for many of her fictional towns). Throughout her career she wrote extensively about her own domestic life: essays and articles for *Woman's Home Companion* and *Good Housekeeping* and *Woman's Day*, work that Jackson later collected and fictionalized as *Life among the Savages*. The domestic work in the house, it is clear, was hers: the cooking, the cleaning, the raising of their children.

The world of *We Have Always Lived in the Castle* is almost entirely domestic. Constance never leaves their home; a journey to the edge of the garden is worth relating to her sister. Merricat ventures into town twice a week, but only ever to satisfy the 'simple need for books and food'. On the edge of society, the sisters have little to do but cook, and eat, and maintain the house.

It is hardly surprising, then, that the narrative is obsessed with food: food as home, food as history, food as threat. Visitors come to the house and refuse to eat, still terrified they may be poisoned. Uncle Julian, who survived the poisoning but lives entirely in the past, mourns that he did not know that the fatal night would be his wife's last; if he had he would have 'permitted her more sausage' at breakfast. Cousin Charles arrives (appearing to charm Constance but clearly after the house) and Merricat sits across the table from him, calmly telling him how she could poison him by putting deadly mushrooms in his dinner. Generations of the family, unnamed great- and great-great-grandmothers, live on in the cellar in the form of jars of preserves that Constance will not allow the others to consume: 'deeply colored rows of jellies and pickles and bottled vegetables and fruit, maroon and amber and dark rich green, stood side by side in our cellar and would stand there forever, a poem by the Blackwood women'.

'Domestic horror' is a term often applied to Jackson's works, a phrase that refers to a 'horror within the family'. But it is important to note that it is not the domesticity, not the cooking or the cleaning, not the relationship between the sisters, that is the horror here. Merricat maintains the boundaries around their house; Constance seems to enjoy cooking (certainly once it is no longer for the whole family) and there's thought and love evident in the menus that she plans; they have joy in the garden and the many small, fresh, delicious things they find in it. 'We eat the year away. We eat the spring and the summer and the fall. We wait for something to grow and then we eat it.'

Nor is the horror here something lurking in the cellar or something supernatural. The horror is in the weight of the home, the conventional patriarchal family structure. It is the social and domestic burden on women. It is the constantly watchful townsfolk, 'their flat grey faces with the hating eyes'. The horror lies in the expectation that the sisters would have to defer to Charles, should he insert himself into their home and find a way to stay. Once Uncle Julian dies, once Cousin Charles accepts he has lost, the last of Constance's obligations are gone. She can live quite happily in the crumbling wreck of the house, needing nothing but her sister. 'Slowly the pattern of our days grew, and shaped itself into a happy life.'

There is a fire, at the end. A fire that hints at witchcraft, not least when an angry mob arrives to throw stones at the sisters and destroy their home as it burns. But it is a fire that Merricat has lit, a fire that cleanses, a fire that pushes Charles out, and allows Constance and Merricat to rebuild their life as they want it. They survive, and so does the kitchen. And once the flames have been extinguished, it seems as if the anger and fury of the townsfolk have been extinguished too. The neighbours, those who, early on in the narrative, use the pretext of coming to tea to stare at the sisters, now arrive to invite them to stay 'until [they] can decide what to do with you'. They're going to 'forget all about' what happened.

Merricat and Constance refuse to be a problem that needs solving. They stay hidden in the wreck, they make soup and onion pie, they scrub a fire-damaged mattress to sleep on, they allow the neighbourhood children to fear them, they take in the culinary offerings the townsfolk leave at their door. After so long living outside defined roles, after six years building their own world of safety, how could anyone imagine they would want to return to conformity? They don't *want* anyone to decide what to do with them.

We Have Always Lived in the Castle was Jackson's last novel (*Nine*

Magic Wishes, an illustrated children's book, was released a year later in 1963). Soon after its publication she had a nervous breakdown; she had 'written myself into the house'. Yet she retained a hope of escaping her life as a faculty wife, of leaving behind the domestic weight and societal expectations she had spent her life writing a way out of: 'The thought of a ring around my finger always made me feel tied tight, because rings had no openings to get out of.' Jackson died in 1965, at the age of 48.

KATE YOUNG is an award-winning writer and cook. She is the author of *The Little Library* series of cookbooks, which take inspiration from literature. Her latest, *The Little Library Parties*, was published in 2022. You can hear her in Episode 32 of our podcast, *'Picnic at Hanging Rock* & Other Stories'.

Completely Foxed

DAVID FLEMING

During late evening strolls round the quiet streets near my home I occasionally have a close encounter with a fox. We stand there, yards apart, each daring the other to move first, till finally the beast will run off up a nearby drive while I continue on my solitary way. There is something mysterious about foxes, and I must confess that I find such meetings slightly alarming.

On a winter afternoon in the year 1880 a newly married couple, Richard and Silvia Tebrick, go for a woodland walk, during which Mrs Tebrick unexpectedly and mysteriously turns into a fox. Mr Tebrick carries his wife home and the couple continue to live together as best they can under these difficult circumstances. But over time, Silvia's new bestial nature takes over from her fading humanity and their prospects become increasingly precarious.

This transformation – established fact according to the author – forms the basis of David Garnett's haunting and intriguing novel *Lady into Fox* which was published to some acclaim in 1922. One of its marvels is that a book so short – fewer than a hundred pages – can be simultaneously a comedy and a tragedy, a biting social satire and a touching love story.

Garnett was a prominent member of the Bloomsbury Group, part of that generation of writers who delighted in attacking the values

David Garnett, *Lady into Fox* (1922)
Dover · Pb · 96pp · £8.99 · ISBN 9780486493190

and social mores of their Victorian predecessors, and the novel can be read as a critique of old-fashioned patriarchal attitudes. Richard Tebrick longs for his vixen to retain the dainty and docile habits formerly displayed by his human wife, and he is tortured by the increasing wildness of her nature and her longing for freedom. When she tries to run off into the surrounding countryside he cries:

> 'Silvia, Silvia, why do you do this? Are you trying to escape from me? I am your husband, and if I keep you confined it is to protect you, not to let you run into danger. Show me how I can make you happy and I will do it, but do not try to escape from me.'

It's a sentiment expressed by men down the ages who fear their 'Angel in the House' will spread her wings and fly away spiritually, sexually or philosophically.

The focus of the novel is on Richard's reaction to his wife's transformation, rather than on Silvia's experience as a fox. He is on an emotional roller-coaster and we share his thoughts, feelings and cries of hope and despair, as he is driven towards the edge of sanity. Sylvia, on the other hand, and for obvious reasons, is silent. We can judge her views only by her actions – as when she uses her newly acquired vixen-like cunning to attempt an escape from a walled garden into the countryside beyond. Of the two, she is the one who adapts to the new situation more readily.

Richard's views may be old-fashioned, but, seeing his torment, we come to admire his loyalty and devotion to his wife. As the story progresses he sheds all decorum and becomes a dishevelled recluse, sleeping under the stars and joining Silvia in her hunting expeditions where he scrabbles about amateurishly on all fours. The sexual implications of the story are lightly touched on. At first the couple continue to share the same bed, but Silvia soon prefers to sleep on the floor. Later, Richard suffers jealousy over the success of his love rival – a local dog fox.

Though so original, *Lady into Fox* had several possible influences, one of which was the wave of nostalgia for rural life that swept the country during and immediately after the First World War. This gave birth to some notable literary works featuring foxes and the people who hunted them – John Masefield's long narrative poem *Reynard the Fox* in 1919 and Siegfried Sassoon's *Memoirs of a Fox-Hunting Man*

in 1928 (see p. 36 of this issue). But the contemporary work with which it has most affinity is Mary Webb's novel of 1917, *Gone to Earth*, in which the main character, Hazel Woodus, keeps a pet vixen and is depicted as a child of Nature identifying with 'all things hunted and snared and destroyed'. Her hair is 'tawny and fox-like', and she is pursued by, among others, the local minister who hopes to make her into a respectable wife. The climactic scenes of the novels are virtually identical, though I won't divulge them here.

What gives *Lady into Fox* a real edge is the witty and ambiguous narration that allows it to be read and reread on so many different levels. Though set in a rural past it's a thoroughly modern novel, and Garnett enters the story himself in the following dry aside:

> I met not long ago with someone who, after talking some little while and not knowing me or who I was, told me that David Garnett was dead, and died of being bitten by a cat after he had tormented it. He had long grown a nuisance to his friends as an exorbitant sponge upon them, and the world was well rid of him.

No doubt this was a private joke – possibly for the amusement of the painter Duncan Grant to whom the book was dedicated – but it also gives our dubious narrator the opportunity to remind us that he has scrupulously avoided rumour and gossip in telling his story and has relied solely on verifiable facts.

Lady into Fox is illustrated with wood engravings by the author's first wife, Rachel Garnett, and they add immeasurably to its charm, being, like the story itself, amusing and oddly sad. The novel was so well-known in its day that it became the subject of a parody by Christopher Ward called *Gentleman into Goose*. Garnett meanwhile went on to write many other books, but he never outshone his startling and brilliant debut.

When not meeting foxes or listening to *The Archers*, DAVID FLEMING is putting the finishing touches to a book about statues, dolls, robots and other types of human simulacra. The illustrations in this article are by Rachel Garnett.

The Man Who Stopped at Nothing

GRANT MCINTYRE

Some writers lead us into lives we'd never otherwise imagine; Michael Herr, writing on the fear and madness of war, was one; Thomas Merton on monastic seclusion, another. Oliver Sacks was one as well. He was an explorer of mind and brain, where words like inconceivable, or magical, or sometimes alas tragic, are not overblown but just plain fact. Everyone's heard of the man, his wife and the hat – but Sacks met many, many others whose lives were just as much sources of wonder. He was open to them because his own experience was extraordinary too. His writings and his life are almost equally absorbing.

He was a big, untidy man, superhumanly strong and awkward; like Tolstoy's Pierre Bezukhov, shy but full of feeling. In the Sacks family, career meant medicine, but for him some options were ruled out straightaway; he was never going to be a surgeon, with what Jonathan Miller – a lifelong friend – called his sheer 'flat-footed Jewish clumsiness'. As for laboratory research, when he absent-mindedly dropped his lunch into a biochemical culture he was firmly ejected. 'You are a menace,' he was told. 'Go and work with patients.'

He was not only large in build, but in compassion and curiosity too, and also in recklessness and self-doubt. Will Self called his life 'an adventure in ideas'. It was one in conflicts as well. His background was orthodox Jewish from Cricklewood, north London; he embraced Jewishness but was still up for startling, un-kosher rebel-

---

Oliver Sacks's *Awakenings* (1973), *The Man Who Mistook His Wife for a Hat* (1985) and his memoir *On the Move* (2015) are all available as Picador paperbacks.

lions like blood milkshakes or fried placentas. 'He stopped at nothing!' said Miller. The Sacks home didn't readily admit gentiles, but his parents were doctors for everyone regardless of belief. In fact they were so dedicated that while they tended the needy during the war they sent their youngest sons out of the way to boarding-school, without noticing that for two years the boys were viciously bullied, abused and beaten. Pleas for rescue were ignored. Oliver's brother became schizophrenic, and he himself lost what he called 'the three Bs, the ability to bond, belong, and believe' – that's believe as in trust. Things were made worse by the fact that he was gay. He wanted it kept secret from his mother; he was her prodigy and she his formidable guide. But she found out, and 'with a face he'd never seen before' cursed him with Old Testament thunder and wished he had not been born. He became hypersensitive to inner life, and an outsider.

Not long after his mother's outburst he left England for internships in America. He was still raw, beyond the usual uncertainty of youth. In those days homosexuality was a crime – Alan Turing's fate was hard to forget. Perhaps it's no surprise he went off the rails and on to drugs. He became a bodybuilder pumping iron on LA's Muscle Beach, and a biker on terms with Hell's Angels. Leaving the ward on a Friday night he'd swallow a handful of amphetamines, then, lying flat on the tank of his monstrous BMW, he'd hurtle through the night at the highest speed it could reach. The headlight and the drugs would create 'all kinds of strange reversals and illusions' as the road sped by. He took refuge in danger like this.

However, he did go and work with patients, and probably they saved him from an early death. He had always been intrigued by consciousness, whether human or other. What was 'I' for a bat, for instance, or an octopus? And, now he was caring for them, what was 'I' for a sleeping-sickness patient unresponsive and rigid for decades? Or for that same patient briefly restored to previous life by L-DOPA? When we look into the wounded consciousness of others, he asked, are we looking at ourselves? Are we frightened to look in the mirror?

The L-DOPA patients were, of course, the subject of *Awakenings* (1973), which first brought him recognition, if not immediately in science then by way of the arts: a film, a play, an opera, a ballet.

Early in his career he sat in on a clinic where a mentally impaired adolescent girl was being assessed. She failed test after test; failures were in fact the whole point of the tests – they charted her limits. By chance he spotted her later in a park and they talked. Immediately he saw that away from the clinic she lived in her own complex imaginative reality – one perhaps not reachable by someone normally able. He realized that difference might not always be just loss. It widened his understanding of what being human is, and formed his approach to patients. For him they were not cases but complete people he knew in depth, combining 'the objectivity of science with the intense sense of fellow feeling, and the sheer wonder, and sometimes tragedy, of it all'. He wrote about them as Dickens or Melville might.

He explored the stupendous powers that sometimes appear in otherwise drastically limited 'savants', like the Lin twins, who couldn't manage arithmetic but who could 'see' prime numbers twenty digits long – which no computer of the time could reveal. Or the nineteenth-century blind black slave boy Tom, scarcely verbal but an excellent self-taught pianist who could also, as a joke, play one tune with his left hand and another with his right, while singing a third. Sacks explored hallucinations too, such as the fairies Conan Doyle saw, or Dostoevsky's personal interviews with God. Or Maupassant's meeting his own double. It's problematic meeting oneself – it may feel unclear which self is hallucinating. Sacks himself, travelling up the Amazon with a fever, found himself in a Jane Austen novel (though he was actually more a Dickens man). If he got up – for some water perhaps – his fellow characters would disappear from sight. When they returned, he'd find the story had moved on without him.

Neurology fast became Sacks's life, though neurology of a kind very out of favour: literary, personally engaged, humanely perceptive. He was both therapist and explorer, fascinated by the vast variety of what our fragile minds can achieve, and by the creative adaptations our brains sometimes have to make for them to do so. He engaged with humanity of every kind. He'd sit till dawn with the damaged and delirious, somehow tuned to their frantic thoughts, and he'd bring comfort. Here's what Sister Lorraine of the Little Sisters of the Poor had to say. (Sacks worked for the Little Sisters for nothing; it was a nursing order so poor the nuns had to beg on the streets of Brooklyn.)

> I look on Our Lord as the Divine Physician and in a way – I hope this is not sacrilege – I look on [the] Doctor in the same way: he heals, but not just the superficial problems, he heals underneath . . . It must be profound experience. It can't be just brilliance.

It's hard to exaggerate how unwelcome his ideas were to scientists sixty years ago, when neurology was doing its best to look like physics. There can't be many doctors more loved by their patients than Oliver Sacks, but he wasn't loved by his colleagues, and in turn he scorned their refusal to swim beyond the shallows of scientific proof. 'They are addicted to their fragmentations, their specializations,' he said. 'They resent creativity.' Not surprisingly he was ignored or accused of making things up. And to be honest he did sometimes transgress; 'I don't tell lies,' he said, 'though I may invent the truth.' He was neurotic about his place in science, swinging between moods of grandiosity and doubt.

The man who mistook his wife for a hat was Dr P, a singing teacher at the Juilliard School who could no longer recognize his students – at least not by their faces, only by their voices. A visit to Dr Sacks was arranged. After an awkward moment when P tried to shake hands with a grandfather clock, Sacks gave him a rose to look at, and waited to see what happened. 'A convoluted red form with a linear green attachment,' P said. But what was it? P guessed only when he took a sniff. Sacks produced something more difficult. 'A continuous surface,' P said after a pause, 'infolded on itself . . . It appears to have five out-pouchings, if that is the word . . . a container of some sort? . . . It could be a change purse . . . for coins of five sizes?' The first thing most of us would see – that it was a glove – was what he couldn't see. Stroke damage had cost him his sense of the 'thingness' of things. That's why he came to reach not for his hat but his wife's head instead.

Amazingly, P had no idea anything was wrong with him. Yet despite that, with his wife's help he'd already adjusted to cope. 'How does he get dressed?' Sacks asked in a quiet moment. 'I put his usual clothes out, in all the usual places, and he dresses without difficulty, singing to himself. He does everything singing to himself. But if he is interrupted . . . he comes to a complete stop, doesn't know his clothes – or his own body . . . He can't do anything unless he makes it a song.' The musical centres of P's brain were in some inexplicable way standing in for the visual.

The Man Who Mistook His Wife for a Hat (1985) was a bestseller in twenty languages. That didn't silence critics; there were jibes about the man who mistook his patients for a literary career. But change was coming. It casts an ironic light on human nature, even the human nature of scientists, that what made most difference was an Oscar-nominated film starring Robin Williams and Robert De Niro. The book *Awakenings* had been met with scorn or silence, but the film of it caught people's imagination. It spread the feeling that 'hopeless cases' could be reached out to, not just categorized and medicated; it created a mood to which not even the most austere and fatalistic neurologists were completely immune. So the tide of Sacks's prestige turned. Outsider became international treasure. I recently read that of students opting to study neurology, 70 per cent now cite Oliver Sacks as the reason. And for readers like ourselves he has opened a new continent.

GRANT MCINTYRE was a publisher and is now a reader.

Looking Horror in the Eye

TIM PEARS

My father was a country priest, a bookish intellectual hidden in a Devon valley on the edge of Dartmoor. He was something of a Russophile, and among the books that lined the walls of his study was a section of Russian literature. I left school at 16, much to his bemusement, and in between odd bouts of employment and moping around like a teenage Oblomov I read through the canon of nineteenth-century Russian novels – they became my nourishment, my writer's seedbed.

After my father's death, and through house moves and the various changing arrangements of life, that Russian section of his library was scattered. With one exception: I held on to his five volumes of *The Story of a Life* by Konstantin Paustovsky. There were various reasons for this. One was that the work was an outlier, a series not of novels but of memoirs, ones covering moreover not the nineteenth century but the first part of the twentieth. A second was their beauty as objects, hardback copies published by Harvill Press. And a third, most significantly, was that I could remember my father reading them, reporting at breakfast the pleasure of his previous evening's immersion. And so I kept them with me, literary totems.

It was some years before I opened the first volume, *Childhood and Schooldays*, and was instantly captivated.

Konstantin or Kostik Paustovsky was born in Moscow in 1893 but

The first three books of Konstantin Paustovsky's *The Story of a Life* (1964–7), translated by Douglas Smith, are available in a single volume: Vintage · Hb · 816pp · £25 · ISBN 9781784873080.

grew up from the age of 5 in Kiev, where his father Georgy was sent for his work as a statistician with the railways. Kostik was the youngest of four, with two older brothers, Boris and Vadim, and a sister, Galya.

Kostik had varied ancestry. His paternal grandfather, descendant of Zhaporidzian Cossacks, was an ox-cart driver. In his youth he'd fought in the Russo-Turkish wars and been captured, but he had somehow returned with a beautiful Turkish wife. As she aged she became increasingly bad-tempered, and he kept out of her way in a hut amongst his beehives, where the grandchildren visited him and he sang them old Cossack songs in a trembling tenor.

Kostik's mother, Maria, was from a noble but impoverished family. His maternal grandfather was a sullen, silent man employed in a sugar factory. His grandmother was Polish, a pious Catholic, who remained in lifelong mourning – not for a loved one but rather for the suppression of the Polish rebellion in 1863.

In 1904 Kostik followed his brothers into the elite First Kiev Gymnasium. Chapters describe the eccentric behaviour of teachers and fellow pupils, who included Mikhail Bulgakov. Outside the school, change was brewing. In October 1905 Tsar Nicholas II issued an imperial manifesto promising civil rights and democratic elections. In Kiev as elsewhere spontaneous celebrations erupted. Kostik and his friends rushed to join in. But first mounted police attacked the crowd, then anti-Semitic violence spread. Thugs roamed the streets. Shortly thereafter his father Georgy abandoned the family for another woman. His mother Maria and his sister Galya left Kiev to join Kostik's brothers, who were now in Moscow. Living in a rented room, Kostik subsidized himself through his last years of school by tutoring.

Volume two, *Slow Approach of Thunder*, opens in 1914, with Paustovsky at Moscow University. As a youngest son and a student, one moreover with poor eyesight, he was spared call-up to the army in the First World War, but as the conflict intensified he abandoned his studies to work first as a tram conductor and then as a medical orderly on a hospital train. Travelling across Russia and Poland and to the Eastern Front, he saw in gruesome detail the savagery and suffering of war. Meanwhile, both his brothers would perish in action. Paustovsky went on to work in an armaments factory, then as a fisherman on the Sea of Azov. Returning to Moscow, he found work as a journalist and was sent out to write about the political currents bubbling in the provinces in the first days of 1917. The book ends with the abdication of the Tsar.

The third volume, *In that Dawn*, opens with Paustovsky careering between meetings, open-air speeches and intense discussions in smoky cafés as the populace argued out the aims of revolution. Paustovsky got trapped in his apartment building in a suburb fought over by the Red Army and military cadets loyal to the Provisional Government. Taken for a cadet in his student coat, he was only saved from a firing squad by the arrival of a Red Army officer who recognized him. Later – even as the Bolsheviks took power, in October – he was taken for a spy by anarchists, and for an anarchist by Bolsheviks, again barely escaping with his life in those febrile times.

In order to support his mother and sister, Paustovsky followed them back to Kiev. The city was surrounded by a chaotic maelstrom of forces battling out the Civil War: the Red Army, the White Army, various Ukrainian nationalist factions as well as Poles and Germans. Paustovsky was twice conscripted and took part in confused fighting as well as a mutiny of his fellow soldiers. When the White Russians under General Denikin occupied Kiev, Paustovsky escaped to Odessa, where he scraped a meagre living on a struggling newspaper.

The translation of the first volumes of *The Story of a Life* was by Michael Duncan and Manya Harari. With Marjorie Villiers, Harari had set up Harvill Press (a combination of their surnames) in 1947 (see *SF* no.13). The first five volumes were published between 1964 and 1969. A sixth joined them in 1974 but never made its way to my father's library. I imagine he simply didn't learn of its existence. As the Ukrainian catastrophe unfolded through 2022, I thought of Konstantin Paustovsky, of his varied ancestry and much-travelled life, and of the richness of Russian culture that Putin and his thugs have been happy to destroy along with so much else.

As chance would have it, in January 2022 the first three volumes, newly translated by Douglas Smith, were published by Vintage Classics in a single edition. Now I had a wonderful excuse to reread them.

Kiev was one of the three intellectual centres of Tsarist Russia, along with Moscow and St Petersburg, and a meeting place of nationalities and religions. Paustovsky's Ukrainian and Russian identities were intermingled. Nicholas II visited his high school: walking along a line of the older boys, the Tsar asked them where they were from – there were Russians, Ukrainians, Poles, Jews – and Kostik said, 'Ukrainian'. Yet shortly before, at the death of Tolstoy, he and his schoolmates had mourned 'the greatest writer in our country'. Later, travelling around Russia as a hospital orderly and then as a journalist, Paustovsky developed a deep love of Russia. But as we read we understand that he is not thinking of Russia as a single, separate country: for this was the age of Empire. In the second volume, his hospital train goes to the Eastern Front. As they cross the river San, Paustovsky observes, 'I was leaving the country for the first time.' This seems incongruous when one has already read of his travels between Ukraine, Russia, Poland and beyond. The significant frontiers in eastern Europe, however, were those between the Russian, Austro-Hungarian, German and Ottoman empires.

The Story of a Life is an invaluable record of momentous events recounted by a witness caught up in them, but it's also history written by a novelist. Konstantin Paustovsky gives the impression of a man who strolled from crisis to catastrophe, who looked horror in the eye without ever losing an enthusiastic innocence and a sweet curiosity.

His service as a hospital orderly was the experience that forged him. He and a nurse, Lolya, fell in love. Near the front line they were sent with another nurse to help a village, which appeared to be protected by units of Russian soldiers. Kostik and Lolya entered the village and found its inhabitants dying from smallpox. The soldiers were in place not to protect the villagers but to stop them escaping. The nurses realized that they themselves were now trapped. All they could do was ease people's suffering and hope they didn't catch the pox themselves. But Lolya came down with the telltale signs. Kostik nursed her, and then buried her at the edge of the village, his heart broken.

Paustovsky had a remarkable eye for detail, or rather his memory did. He claimed that one should never rely on notes, for then one does not fully inhabit existence but merely observes it. Instead, the memoirist should return to past events and allow memory to make its own, superior, selection. No doubt this was as disingenuous as most writers' pronouncements on their work. The translator Douglas Smith describes finding Paustovsky's work in Moscow archives: to his surprise the lucid prose of the finished work was achieved through laborious handwritten drafts, with so many crossings-out, amendments and other scrawls as to render the work almost illegible.

But if there is any truth in Paustovsky's dictum, then his memory was forensic. He describes falling in love at the age of 9, with 16-year-old Hannah:

> She braided orange and black ribbons in her thick reddish plaits. Around her neck hung a necklace of dull coral. Hannah had sparkling, greenish eyes. Every time Hannah smiled, she lowered her eyes and then raised them slowly as if they were too heavy to lift.

During the war, attached to a field dressing station,

> Twice we stopped to bury dead bodies abandoned by the roadside . . . one was a young peasant woman. Her light-coloured eyes were still open, and she looked up peacefully into the sky where a yellow sun shone through the smoke. A bee, entangled in the woman's hair, buzzed angrily.

There are countless descriptions of nature, and of the passing scene, like this one from his hospital train: 'Tall black crucifixes stood at the crossroads. Old women with their knitting sat beside them, and tethered goats grazed on the grass. Candles burned in a small chapel, but I could not make out anyone inside.'

By taking time to notice incidental detail in every scene, Paustovsky achieves the paradoxical effect of creating a slow reading pace of material that teems with colour and incident. He also depicts people imbued with the peculiarities of their epoch – of dress, behaviour, thought – while always noting the human qualities that render them as familiar as our own friends or neighbours. Rumyantsev is a soldier friend of his uncle's.

> It wasn't easy to get a good look at him. He was always hidden behind clouds of tobacco smoke and was so shy he preferred to sit in the darkest corners of the living room. There he would sit hunched over a chessboard absorbed in a problem. If he suc-

ceeded in solving it, he broke out in laughter and rubbed his
hands.

In his thirties, Paustovsky settled down to the life of a writer and,
despite never joining the Communist Party or taking part in denun-
ciations of others (indeed in later life he went out of his way to
defend and promote writers in trouble), he became a successful novelist in Stalin's Soviet Union. In his fifties he began work on these
memoirs for which he is best remembered.

At the end of the third volume, as Soviet troops approach Odessa,
White Russians rush to steamships in the harbour. Paustovsky looks
down from Alexandrovsky Park upon the crowd pressing desperately
up the gangplanks.

I saw one lucky man take hold of the railing only to be immediately clutched at by many hands. He inched his way forward,
dragging these people along with him up the gangway, but then
lost his hold and fell together with the others still clinging to
his body into the sea. Unable to free himself from this terrible
human load, he went down into the water and disappeared.

It was 1917, but such is the freshness of Paustovsky's observation,
and the repetitions of history, that it could have been yesterday. And
it could be tomorrow.

TIM PEARS is the author of eleven novels, most recently the *West Country Trilogy*
(2017–19) and the collection *Chemistry and Other Stories* (2021). His novel *Run
to the Western Shore* is due in November from Swift Press. You can hear him in
Episode 19 of our podcast, 'Tim Pears's West Country'.

Gone Away!

FLORA WATKINS

Can you recall the novel that took you away from the nursery book-shelves and into the realms of Grown-Up Books – a gateway book, if you like? I happened upon mine after months of resisting efforts both at home and at school to get me to read something more challenging. Until then, as a pony-mad child without a pony, I'd sought refuge in my tattered copies of thrilling stories like *Show-Jumping Secret* and *We Hunted Hounds* by the Pullein-Thompson sisters. Then one day, entirely of my own volition, when I was perhaps 12 or 13, I reached for the blue, cloth-bound copy of Siegfried Sassoon's *Memoirs of a Fox-Hunting Man.*

Most readers encounter Sassoon as the brave soldier-poet with the Military Cross, the mentor of Wilfred Owen, who has shaped our thinking on the First World War perhaps more than anyone else. It was Sassoon who first exposed the horrors of the trenches in his poetry. His depiction of the calamitous Western Front and the gulf between blundering, incompetent generals and innocent young soldiers betrayed is the overriding impression we have of that conflict, despite efforts of revisionist historians in the decades since his death. But that afternoon, as I devoured the first of Sassoon's three volumes of lightly fictionalized autobiography, I met him as a boy in the person of his alter-ego George Sherston, clip-clopping to a distant meet alongside Dixon the groom, his fingers numb and a melting hoarfrost on the hedgerows.

Siegfried Sassoon, *Memoirs of a Fox-Hunting Man* (1928)
Faber · Pb · 320pp · £9.99 · ISBN 9780571322831

Sassoon began *Memoirs of a Fox-Hunting Man* (1928) as the spoof reminiscences of a retired sporting colonel living in Cheltenham. But in the autumn of 1926 he destroyed these and, using his hunting memories to escape an unhappy present (he had burnt much of his recent poetry and was in an unsatisfactory relationship with a young actor), he began to write about a boy growing up in Kent.

George Sherston (a surname taken from a village in the famous Beaufort Hunt country) is a shy, sensitive, rather lonely boy, raised by a maiden aunt in a Wealden village. Like Sherston when the book opens, I had never 'seen hounds', as hunting people say, and hunting terminology was a mystery to me. I'd no idea that a 'ratcatcher' was a tweed coat worn before the opening meet, that 'covert' has a silent 't', or that 'holloa' – the shriek emitted when the quarry is spotted leaving the covert – is pronounced 'holler'.

Under the guidance of Dixon, who is keen to make a proper little fox-hunting man of his young charge, I thrilled with Sherston to the excitement of the chase, the anticipation aroused by a nip in the air which means that hounds will 'run like the blazes . . . fairly scream along' (scent, Dixon explains, is most pungent on cold, damp ground). I was there with him at his very first meet, riding pillion on his little cob, Sheila:

And then, for the first time, I heard a sound which has thrilled generations of foxhunters to their marrow. From the far side of the wood came the long shrill screech (for which it is impossible to find an adequate word) which signifies that one of the whips has viewed the fox quitting the covert. 'Gone Away' it meant. But before I had formulated the haziest notion about it, Lord Dumborough was galloping up the ride and the rest of them were pelting after him as though nothing could stop them . . .

Despite Sherston's obsession with the chase, for the reader who does not share his passion he is never boring. *Memoirs of a Fox-Hunting Man* is a lyrical evocation of a vanished, unspoilt rural England, a eulogy for the Elysian Weald of Sassoon's youth. Here, during those gorgeously golden Edwardian summers before the First World War, we meet Aunt Evelyn, with smelling salts in hand and a bee veil over her head, her world limited by 'the distance she could cover in a four-wheeled dog cart' and divided into people whom one could 'call on' and people who were 'socially impossible'. There are sleek-haired little boys in Eton jackets, a stationmaster in a top hat and a baggy black frockcoat, and at home a 'fire-lit parlour' and 'the smell of strawberry jam'.

From this Utopia Sassoon excised unhappy elements of his own boyhood: the scandal of his father leaving his mother and her mental instability. In his 2005 biography Max Egremont writes of Sassoon becoming 'more English' in *Fox-Hunting Man*, of 'purging' that which had set him apart from his contemporaries – his homosexuality and his Jewishness. The adult Sherston acknowledges that memory is imperfect, that it reflects like the tarnished mirror in the sunless passage that led to his schoolroom. He admits to the reader that he is 'reconstructing' his life as he loiters among his memories, recasting and reimagining. Recalling the cricket match at the annual village flower show, he confesses: 'The umpires are in their place. But it is in the sunshine of my own clarified retrospection that they are wearing their white coats.'

But Sassoon's own 'clarified retrospection' is far more radical than Sherston's, with his homosexuality expunged entirely. While writing the book, he became enmeshed in a torrid, protracted affair with the aesthete Stephen Tennant. Later he would embark on marriage to a young woman called Hester Gatty, who was twenty years his junior. He saw her as the chance to 'redeem my life'; the marriage was, inevitably, disastrous.

The reader might sense Sassoon's true feelings in Sherston's intense friendship with the fictional Stephen Colwood – in reality Stephen Gordon Harbord, the son of a sporting parson whose vicarage became Sassoon's second home – and with Denis Milden, the name he gave to Norman Loder, an expert Old Etonian huntsman and his boyhood hero. The companionable scenes when Sherston goes to stay at the kennels with Denis – 'the most significant occasion my little world could offer me' – have the easy familiarity of a contented married couple:

> It was after half-past six when he came in. He seemed to take me for granted already, but assured me again he was 'terrible pleased to have someone to talk to'. . . As soon as he had swallowed a cup of tea he lit his pipe and sat down at his writing-table to open a pile of letters.

The war does not intrude on this idyll until late in the book, when Sherston's innocence and naïvety, and the world he has evoked, are shattered. Sassoon would give a fuller account of his experiences in the trenches in *Memoirs of an Infantry Officer* (1930), completing the trilogy with *Sherston's Progress* (1936), which begins with his arrival at Slateford War Hospital, based on Craiglockhart, a sanatorium in Edinburgh. Sassoon was sent there by an army medical board in July 1917, diagnosed with shell shock and a nervous breakdown after issuing an anti-war statement that was read out in the House of Commons. Wilfred Owen, a fellow in-patient, sought out his company; Sassoon would suggest changes to 'Anthem for Doomed Youth' and help him get published.

In the closing pages of *Memoirs* there is a clarion call, as great as anything Orwell wrote in response to the Second World War, for a certain kind of England, for the 'pleasant and homely countrified life . . . I wanted the past to survive and to begin again'. Sassoon writes with the same lyricism on the hell of Flanders as he does on the Elysian fields of the Weald. Under bombardment, 'the sky winked and flickered like a thunderstorm gone crazy' with 'a remote rumble . . . like heavy furniture being moved about in a room overhead'. Here in the trenches it is hunting that sustains Sherston, whether he is daydreaming or indulging in 'sporting make-believe':

> Assuming a Denis Milden manner . . . I would go solemnly through a wood, cheering imaginary hounds. After an imaginary fox had been found, away we'd scuttle, looking in vain for a fence to jump, making imaginary casts after an imaginary check, and losing our fox when the horses had done enough galloping. An imaginary kill didn't appeal to me, somehow.

Some names and details from Sassoon's real hunting world are unchanged, or only altered very slightly. Sherston's noble hunter Cockbird, on which he wins the Colonel's Cup at a point-to-point, was a real horse, winning several races before the war for his proud owner. No doubt the amateur huntsman of the staghounds, Harry Buckman (Buckland in real life), did 'tit-tup stylishly' past Sassoon at a meet, 'his velvet cap cocked slightly over one ear'. When I left BBC News for a staff job at *Horse & Hound* magazine – an unusual move that may owe something to my adolescent reading of Sassoon – one of the first people I met was Buckland's great-great-granddaughter, Lucinda Sims. I had booked myself into one of her hunting clinics to try to fill in the gaps in my knowledge and learn how to 'cross the country' on a horse.

As it turned out there was no need to prise me away from the nursery bookshelves; I was immediately captured by the story of Sassoon's growing up, and by his characters both real and imagined. I have much to thank him for; writing on the first really cold day of the year, in the midst of an energy crisis, I remember Sherston's observation, that no one who understands the significance of a nip in the air ever 'dreads the dark winter'.

FLORA WATKINS first saw hounds in her thirties. She has hunted with several packs but has yet to find her equivalent of Cockbird, Sassoon's hunter of a lifetime.

Boiled Beef and Icy Bedrooms

ROGER HUDSON

In her long reign, stretching across eight decades, Queen Victoria had the support of a number of able and devoted courtiers. They helped her both to adapt to the alterations and accelerations during an era of great change and to serve as a centrepiece and anchor, preserving continuity and dispensing security. They had also, it must be said, to fall in with her demanding, often selfish style of living with its rigidly imposed and often tedious routines. And they had to find ways of softening and adjusting her more irrational or intemperate commands, reprimands and refusals. One must hope that a few of the courtiers who have come and gone during her great-great-granddaughter's even longer reign also wrote letters or kept diaries. Then one day we may be as entertained and enlightened by them as by those that follow.

We turn first to Sarah, Lady Lyttelton. Recently widowed, she came to Windsor as a lady-in-waiting in 1838, when she was 50 and Victoria was 19, and one year into her reign. She soon realized that the Queen's memory, as well as her 'eyes, nose and ears, nothing escapes ever'. Her particular duties were to look after the maids of honour, 'and to do the honours of the Castle to strangers, according to their dignity'. She was surprised by the royal 'walk-about' after

---

Correspondence of Sarah Spencer, Lady Lyttelton (1912); Arthur Ponsonby, *Henry Ponsonby, His Life from His Letters* (1942); Victor Mallet (ed.), *Life with Queen Victoria, Marie Mallet's Letters from Court* (1968); and Mary Lutyens (ed.), *Lady Lytton's Court Diary* (1961) are all out of print, but we can obtain second-hand copies.

church on Sunday, the people pressing upon the Queen until 'her courtiers just tap them back and make way for her'. She had to learn to cope with the clutter with which the Queen surrounded herself, going to a play with 'four different wraps, a bouquet, and a bag and an opera glass'. But this was nothing compared to the trials of a state occasion, the prorogation of Parliament, when she had to unpin a diamond diadem and pin in its place on the Queen's head a 12-lb crown, and then do all that in reverse.

In 1842 Lady Lyttelton took on a new role, as governess to Victoria and Albert's children: Vicky, future Empress of Germany, arrived in 1840, Edward, Prince of Wales in 1841, followed by five more by 1850, the year when she retired. Her duties were to keep the French, German and English governesses under her up to the mark, as well as what she called 'my professional business – accounts, tradesmen's letters, maids' quarrels, bad fitting of frocks, desirableness of rhubarb and magnesia, and by way of intellectual pursuits, false French genders and elements of the multiplication table'. One bitter December day she asked Prince Albert to check her accounts and he replied, 'Yes, certainly, if you will consent to my doing reel steps all the time to warm myself.'

The Prince of Wales she considered 'most promising for kindness and nobleness of mind', a judgement which does not say anything for how he was handled by his parents in later years. Vicky had all the intellect of her father but was wilful to a degree. In 1846 'she was most tender and touching in her regrets at leaving me and if at the last minute she had not quarrelled with her bonnet and tried to bite my hand in her rage, I should have taken it for steady affection.' A year later, in September, Lady Lyttelton remarked, 'formidably satirical her turn is – no ridicule or foible escapes her'; then in October, 'If not seen but only overheard, she might pass for a young lady of 17 in whichever of her three languages she chose to entertain the company.' She was regularly punished by being confined to her room, and then her brother would come and cheer her up through the door.

Much time was spent at the new royal residence of Osborne on the Isle of Wight where one afternoon Lady Lyttelton saw 'patches of children each attended by their scarlet footmen . . . the Prince very busy with the builders, the equerries charging about'. The annual fête there was less appealing: 'in the middle of the interminable country dance on the green, nothing but footmen and housemaids pounding away their ale, and the yachts' crews running in sacks and dancing hornpipes'. Occasionally she was required to 'dine down' and eat with the royal couple, once 'to help work off the old Duke of Cambridge [a son of George III]. Tends to ask questions like, "How do you get on here? Rather dull, hey?" within two chairs of the Queen's, at a small table.'

Aristocratic intermarriage, particularly among Whig families, means we should not be surprised that the next figure, Sir Henry Ponsonby (b. 1825), was related to Lady Lyttelton: her aunt Lady Bessborough was Ponsonby's grandmother. He served in the Grenadier Guards, but also as secretary to several lord-lieutenants in Ireland, and in 1857 he became an equerry to Prince Albert. His first royal dinner at Windsor was an ordeal, sitting next to a lady in black: he knew she was a foreign princess but no more than that. By the fish course she still had not uttered so he tried a sentence in English, ending in 'mum'. 'It succeeded and we got on very well . . . After dinner is very awful. We all stand jammed against a wall and our observations are necessarily few.' In 1861 he became equerry to the Queen and married Mary Bulteel, one of her maids of honour, who was also a granddaughter of Lord Grey of the Great Reform Bill. In 1870 it was his wife's uncle, General Grey, whom he succeeded as the Queen's Private Secretary, and this he remained until 1895.

It was as well that this wise and temperate man, endowed with both a sense of proportion and a sense of humour as well as great diplomatic skill, came when he did. Grey had become increasingly rattled by the Queen's infatuation with her Highland servant, John Brown, imagining the worst and fearing it would lead to the end of the monarchy. The Queen, for her part, was becoming increasingly irrational and unbiddable, refusing to carry out public duties, battened down in Balmoral or Osborne, perhaps in the grip of the menopause. She was testing the loyalty of her subjects at a time when the atmosphere was full of demands for reform.

Ponsonby made clear his technique for dealing with the Queen in two passages. 'Of course if I had been a brave able clever man, I might have read her a lecture on her duties. But of course I did nothing of the sort. Had I done so, I suppose I should never have the subject approached again.' Then: 'When she insists that 2 and 2 make 5 I say I cannot help thinking they make 4. She replies there may be some truth in what I say, but she knows they make 5. Thereupon I drop the discussion. It is of no consequence and I leave it there, knowing the fact.' As his son Arthur commented in his life of his father, 'Ponsonby trusted in fact to her good sense, of which he had quite a high opinion, eventually straightening things out. But she must not be bullied into a confession of error.' In 1880 his father gave a typical example of just this:

> The Queen asked me who should represent her [at the funeral of the Empress of Russia]. I said the Duke of Edinburgh [the Queen's second son, Alfred]. The Queen said, 'No, of course he couldn't.' I said, 'Of course he couldn't.' But as I did not know why, I got back to him in the course of conversation and said it was a pity he couldn't. So she telegraphed to ask him if he could and he said he would.

Like everyone else in attendance at Balmoral, Ponsonby had to submit to the strict regime, for instance not being allowed to go out in the morning before the Queen. He had to endure the freezing dining- and drawing-rooms – only the passages had heating. The Queen's circulation was unlike others', and she positively enjoyed the cold – 'I always feel so brisk,' she said. The boredom was often stultifying and sometimes he was reduced to starting an argument just to get a discussion going. The ghillies' balls, where the Queen danced with John Brown, were too rough-and-tumble, with too much hooting and shouting, for his taste. Brown made many enemies through his coarseness and brusque manner, but Ponsonby knew he had to work with him for the Queen's sake.

Our third courtier, Marie Mallet, became a maid of honour in 1887 and later a lady-in-waiting and secretary, following her mother, who had been a woman of the bedchamber, and joining her waggish uncle Alick Yorke, organizer of the theatricals so enjoyed by the Queen. At Balmoral she only ever felt warm in bed, resented the regular bouts of mourning insisted on – 'relapsing into jet, the crêpe pall descending' – but enjoyed her walks alongside the Queen's pony chair because 'One can talk so much more easily.' Once, to her 'intense astonishment, the Queen ascended a huge ladder in order to mount a horse twenty-six years old'.

She recorded a particular instance of the Queen's preoccupation with the trappings of death, even when on holiday at Grasse in the South of France in 1891. A trip was made to the cemetery 'to visit the tombs of various friends. The gentlemen went in a separate carriage full to overflowing with wreaths for the favoured tombs.' She also observed the Queen's eating habits closely: 'Her favourite fruits were oranges, pears and monster indigestible apples which would have daunted most people half her age but she enjoyed them, sometimes sharing a mammoth specimen with Princess Beatrice . . . The service was so rapid that a slow eater like myself or Mr Gladstone never had time to finish even a most moderate helping.' After dinner,

At eleven p.m. the Queen leaves the drawing-room and I wait in my bedroom until I am summoned and go to the Queen in her sitting-room where I talk and read and take orders until about half-past-twelve, then 'good night' . . . This routine never varies by a hair's-breadth; as soon a revolution as to drive in the morning and walk after lunch, and boiled beef on Thursday and mehlspeise mit ananas [pudding with pineapple] on Friday recur with unfailing regularity.

Marie had things to say about the Queen's daughters: Beatrice, the youngest, was 'unsympathetic and self-absorbed'; Christian (Helena), 'indiscreet but the greatest comfort'; Louise, 'Never have I come across a more dangerous woman. To gain her end she would stick at nothing.' Vicky, the Empress Frederick, was 'tactless but very intelligent'. When she argued with her mother, 'It was most amusing to see two people who are never contradicted, playing the game with each other.' And of the Queen herself? 'What an angel she is and how little she knows of the world we poor mortals inhabit.'

The last figure is Lady Lytton, an impoverished former Vicereine of India (and a cousin of Marie Mallet). She was on duty when the new Tsar Nicholas II of Russia and his wife Alix came to visit Balmoral in 1896. Nicholas resented being forced to go shooting in bad weather by his uncle, the Prince of Wales, especially since he only got two grouse and no stags, but he left £1,000 as a tip and said the Queen 'was kinder and more amiable than ever'. Lady Lytton found that the Queen walked up a plank to get into her carriage for her long afternoon drives, which were testing, even if broken by a lavish tea in a keeper's cottage; on them the Queen gave out gifts of dress material to the deserving poor. When the Queen finally died at Osborne in 1901, it is claimed the Kaiser measured her for her coffin, and the London prostitutes wore black. What is true is that Lady Lytton found herself discharging her last duty alone, except for another lady-in-waiting 'and five admirals', with the coffin on board ship steaming to the mainland.

ROGER HUDSON remains amazed that he was born only forty-two years after Queen Victoria's death.

Cooking with Confidence

OLIVIA POTTS

The day before I sit down to write this piece, I am having lunch with my husband's family. For pudding, Auntie Chris serves up her Christmas pudding. It is undoubtedly *hers* – always made to the same recipe, she tells us, the recipe her mother used before her. 'I use the same one,' her daughter chimes in. But of course, the recipe is also Marguerite Patten's. What follows is warmth, recognition, even gratitude for a recipe that has become part of this family, woven into its years and celebrations. Quickly, everyone around the table admits to having a copy of Patten's seminal book, *Cookery in Colour* – a book so ubiquitous that its now dated cover is almost instantly recognizable on a shelf.

It is no exaggeration to say that Patten taught multiple generations to cook. Her cookbooks bear little resemblance to the celebrated cookbooks of today: they were real manuals, designed to teach basic cooking, even (often especially) for those short on time, money, energy or knowledge. But they were no flash in the pan: Patten's step-by-step, no-nonsense pragmatism won over countless readers. She became a fixture of our kitchens, her recipes adopted by families as their own, and passed on like an inheritance.

Marguerite Patten was born Hilda Elsie Marguerite Brown in Bath in 1915. Her father died in 1927 when she was 12, leaving her mother to bring up three children of whom she was the eldest. 'I am frequently asked if I enjoyed cooking from an early age, and the

---

Marguerite Patten, *Cookery in Colour* (1960), is out of print, but we can obtain second-hand copies. Many of her other books are still in print.

answer is "No",' she said later in life, but she began cooking occasionally to help her busy mother after her father's death. She had ambitions as an actress and spent a season in repertory in Oldham after leaving school. During her first 'resting' period she took a job with the Frigidaire Appliance Company, demonstrating to customers how to use their new refrigerator for cooking. The role required a sense of performance that captured Patten's imagination and sent her down the path of home economy.

During the war she worked for the Ministry of Food, creating and promoting recipes which made the most of rationing. She was placed in Harrods, where she gave frequent cookery demonstrations. It was here that she began creating her own dishes and recipes, and writing Harrods-branded cookery books. During this time she also began to appear on BBC radio, first for their daily *Kitchen Front* series and later for a new afternoon programme, *Woman's Hour*. Television followed, and it cemented her role as a kitchen agony aunt.

Her first two non-Harrods cookbooks were explicitly aimed at those who came to the kitchen without prior knowledge. *Learning to Cook* was written for young people who had been unable to learn to cook because of wartime food shortages, and *Cooking for Bachelors and Bachelor Girls* was for young men and women returning from the services and moving away from the family home. This straightforward novice guidance set the tone for the rest of her career.

Her most successful book was *Cookery in Colour* which, at the time, was ground-breaking. Published by Hamlyn in 1960, this 'picture encyclopaedia for every occasion' was the first widely available cookbook containing colour photographs and featured a thousand recipes, almost all of them accompanied by a photo. The idea was to help the nervous cook by supplying clear visual aids. It was, as you would hope, a riot of colour: so many photos, of course – half a dozen across double-page spreads, and whole pages devoted to pictures of bowls of soup and jars of marmalade – and even those pages full of text and recipes were printed on coloured paper. It was a kaleidoscope of cookery and produce, and full of enthusiasm and abundance. When it was first released, it must have been a staggering sight. And there was undoubtedly a market for it: it sold over 2 million copies.

Over the following fifty years, Patten's output was unparalleled. To describe her as prolific would be an understatement: she wrote 170 cookbooks, including a series of '500' books, all of which featured 500 recipes on a chosen topic (bread and scones, jams, pickles and chutneys, electric mixers and blenders, and so on). Those writers we think of as being the most productive didn't come close to Patten: even including posthumous publications and anthologies of her work, Elizabeth David wrote fewer than 20 books, and Jane Grigson no more than 25. Patten's work sold more than 17 million copies. So perhaps it is no surprise that just about every household in the UK seems to have a copy of a Marguerite Patten book.

Cookery in Colour, like all her books, is spare in its prose. It is there to do a job: to provide comprehensive instruction on all the kinds of cookery that a normal household might want. Her introduction to the Eggs and Cheese chapter reads simply: 'Cheese and eggs are a first-class food. A meal containing cheese or eggs is every bit as nutritious as one with meat or fish. There are so many different cheeses to choose from that dishes need never be monotonous.' She then launches into a dozen recipes that combine eggs and cheese, from a camembert mousse to 'tomato and cheese surprises' (tomatoes stuffed 'tightly' with cheese, panéd and baked). As someone who spends much of her working life faffing about with the words that surround a recipe, it seems to me that Patten has said all that really needs to be said about the marriage of eggs and cheese.

There is an understandable tendency to celebrate those food writers of the twentieth century who wrote discursively or narratively or who – like Claudia Roden or Madhur Jaffrey – introduced new flavours, techniques or cuisines to the UK. But the cookery book as an instructional book deserves its own praise.

Patten was under no illusions about her role. Reading Elizabeth David made her realize that one can tell people about the place in which a dish originated as well as the dish itself: 'I would quite like to do more of that kind of writing but I suppose I'm associated with practicalities, and publishers do tend to put you in pigeon-holes, but maybe that's right because we each have our place. I'm basically not a person who writes a lot about recipes.'

Our engagement with cookbooks has changed since her day: now recipes are widely available (for free) on the Internet, so cookbooks have to offer more than just recipes. They have become physical objects that combine decoration and aspiration, books that include the types of dishes we would like to make – if only we had the time and energy and inclination. Owning one of these books speaks to the kind of person we are or, more accurately, would like to be. We want to be thought of as the person who cooks regularly from Ottolenghi or Alison Roman or Simon Rogan. So it's ironic that the very first cookbook to feature colour photography was so prosaic in its goals and in its target audience.

Each of Patten's books is simply designed to make cooking as easy as possible and she assumes a truly basic level of knowledge or skill. In the breakfast chapter of *The Basic, Basic Cookbook*, she teaches the reader the role of cereal, how to make toast, tea and coffee, and heat up bought bread rolls and tinned baked beans. There is something refreshing about being taken back to basics, with no room for nerves or self-doubt. It is hard to overestimate the value of gentle but firm encouragement: 'Often the basic cook is put off making sauces because people imply they are very difficult. Some sauces are complicated but the recipes that follow are not.'

For the intimidated cook, she is a culinary guardian angel: 'Do not be frightened by the mention of yeast if you have not used it before, as it is very straightforward.' All she really wants is for her readers to find confidence in their kitchens and with food. Alongside her functional language, she encourages curiosity in a delightful way: 'You will find there is an almost bewildering selection of cheeses in good supermarkets and grocers. Occasionally you may be offered a taste of an unfamiliar cheese – do take advantage of this.'

I find Marguerite Patten endlessly reassuring. In *The Basic, Basic Cookbook*, she writes, 'Do not be afraid of entertaining your friends, even if you are a beginner at cooking. It is you they have come to see, they are not judging your culinary skills.' Many of us, myself included, would do well to take her words to heart.

Patten is often written about as a home economist, a celebrity chef (a title she hated: 'I am NOT! To the day I die I'll be a home economist'), a recipe writer, or as a presenter of food. I'm not sure any of these roles truly encapsulates her essence. For me, Patten is quite clearly a teacher. That is the unifying theme throughout her career, from the day she started at Frigidaire to the moment she stopped writing: her many, many cookbooks are testament to a life spent teaching countless readers and children of readers and grandchildren of readers how to cook simply and with confidence.

She died in 2015, aged 99. On hearing of her death, *Woman's Hour* presenter Jane Garvey said, 'Before everyone else there was Marguerite Patten.'

OLIVIA POTTS is a writer and cook. Her first book, *A Half Baked Idea*, won the Fortnum & Mason debut food writing award, and her second book, *Butter: A Celebration*, is out now. You can hear her in Episode 23 of our podcast, 'A Writer in the Kitchen'.

Too Sharp for Her Own Good

CHRIS SAUNDERS

Stella Gibbons is hardly a forgotten writer, but she wrote more for-gotten works than almost anyone else. Her first book, *Cold Comfort Farm* (1940: see *SF* no.10), has a secure and well-deserved place in the literary pantheon – it is a funny, sharp, tender and hugely quot-able novel. Nothing else she wrote equalled its popularity, even the sequels, and by the turn of the millennium it was pretty much the only Gibbons book, out of twenty-five novels, three collections of short stories and four volumes of poems, left in print.

Thanks, however, to the visionary editorial policy of Vintage Classics, a number of Gibbons's works, including *Westwood*, were rescued from obscurity in 2011 in a rather lovely series of paperbacks. *Westwood* in particular was a revelation. *Cold Comfort Farm* is a bril-liant literary satire, taking well-aimed pot-shots at gloomy rural romantic literature. *Westwood*, originally published in 1946, expands Gibbons's project of lampooning literary pretension and this time makes it personal. It is simultaneously a beautiful, tender novel about the disappointments of love and a jaw-dropping skewering of one man, and that unfortunate man is the once celebrated playwright and novelist Charles Morgan.

Morgan was at his peak in the 1930s and '40s, producing hit plays such as *The Flashing Stream* and well-regarded novels including *The Fountain* and *Sparkenbroke*. All his works were characterized by a certain seriousness – as he said himself, his main themes were 'Art,

Stella Gibbons, *Westwood* (1946)
Vintage · Pb · 464pp · £9.99 · ISBN 9780099528722

Love and Death'. T. S. Eliot was a friend and admirer, and in 1936 Morgan was awarded the *Légion d'honneur*. He wore his high seriousness with great pride. In a review for *The Times* of a 1977 revival of his play *The River Line*, Libby Purves uncovered a quote of Morgan's that gives a taste of his authorial personality: 'The sense of humour by which we are ruled avoids emotion, vision and grandeur of spirit as a weevil avoids the sun.' The fact that he was not a bundle of laughs was not lost on his friends. May we all avoid the kind of eulogy that Edith Sitwell gave at Morgan's funeral in 1958: 'Nobility and a sense of fun do not, alas, always go together.'

Morgan's critical success seems to have enraged Stella Gibbons. There is no evidence that she ever met him but, according to her nephew and biographer Reggie Oliver, she took a huge dislike to him and started referring to him privately as 'Charlie-Morgan-Play-the-Organ' as a nod to his preachiness. This could partly have been professional jealousy: Gibbons was never lionized as Morgan was. She sat sniping from the fringes of the literary establishment and so should not have been surprised that it never took her to its heart. However, what was doubly galling to her was the fact that prizes were being lavished upon so po-faced a writer. When she needed a model for Gerard Challis, the sanctimonious, hypocritical villain of *Westwood*, she didn't have far to look.

The novel concerns two friends in wartime London. Hilda prevails through wit, charm, common sense and an enormous well of pragmatism, even more pronounced than in Flora Poste of *Cold Comfort Farm*. She happily entertains a number of men, having no time for romance but plenty for fun. Margaret, on the other hand, is from entirely different stock, and forms the emotional heart of the novel. As a shy, reserved English teacher, not particularly charming or dramatic or clever or, as the reader is regularly reminded, attractive, she would have found no place at Cold Comfort Farm. She falls in with the intelligentsia of 1940s Hampstead and Highgate, which includes Gerard Challis. Margaret is soon in love with the handsome, noble-seeming Challis, whose idea of a seductive line in one of his plays is 'Your ankle bone is softly modelled.' He has no time for coarseness or lust, despite his many marital infidelities, because he is in search of the Ideal Woman:

> Each time he met a woman who seriously attracted him, he put her on her mettle by indicating that he had never met his Ideal Woman outside his own plays, and then she would try to be fiery and dewy, until the inevitable moment arrived when she had had it.

In other words, Challis doesn't like women very much.

History is tight-lipped about Morgan's own sexual affairs, but certainly his novels and plays show his male characters forever in pursuit of the great female lover whose main purpose is to enable them to achieve their full manly potential. For instance, in *The Judge's Story* (1947), the reader is supposed to pity the main character Henry, who neglects his wife Vivien because she is not supportive of his higher calling: 'His enthusiasm, which would in the past have delighted her, even his hard work and moderation of life which her gladness might have rewarded, struck no warmth from her.' Women in Morgan's world, as in Challis's, are at best high priestesses at the altar of male nobility.

Understandably, Gibbons cavils at all this humbuggery, and punishes Challis by making him fall in love with Hilda. Even as she does so, she skewers his pretension. It turns out that Hilda's lack of interest in the noble ideal is greatly mitigated by her extreme prettiness, and this induces in Challis a moment of uncharacteristic self-doubt. He wonders that he should have allowed himself to feel for a girl unlike 'all his other little girls . . . [who] had admired the novels of Charles Morgan or quoted by heart the poems of T. S. Eliot'. It is particularly daring that she directly refers to Morgan and his chum Eliot, inviting the comparison of Challis with the real-life Highgate highbrows.

There is no mistaking her target at this most uncomfortable point in the proceedings.

It just gets worse for Challis. For a start, Hilda never knows his real name, as he has rather ignobly been calling himself Marcus to hide his married status. He takes her to Kew to declare his love – something he has never plighted to his previous girls – and can barely speak: 'for all his fame and all his genius, [he] gazed at her and swallowed convulsively, twice'. When he finally blurts it out, her response is a wonderfully deadpan 'What? . . . Pardon?' Gibbons then adds insult to injury. Challis's grandchildren unexpectedly show up, accompanied by Margaret.

The very seriousness on which Challis's reputation is based forces him to act ridiculously; his life must be lived at the highest pitch of drama because he sees himself as a tragic artist. Hilda's refusal to be anybody's muse completely punctures that particular balloon. In a further irony Margaret, who has hitherto shared Challis's lofty view of himself and who would have been receptive to his advances, loses all respect for him as he chases fruitlessly after the utterly indifferent Hilda. The revelation of Challis's love for Hilda only serves to bring the two women closer together as they realize how shallow he is. As far as Gibbons is concerned, Gerard Challis and Charles Morgan are both done for.

There is a final tension, though. *Westwood*'s subtitle is the *The Gentle Powers*. Towards the end of the novel, after Challis's disastrous declaration of love, Margaret has a discussion with the playwright's mother that cements her rejection of the tragic muse. Margaret says that it seems 'silly and weak' to want to be happy, and Lady Challis gently rebukes her: 'I don't think that you are one of the people who need tragedy. You need what I call the Gentle Powers . . . Beauty, and Time, and the Past and Pity . . . Laughter, too.'

Margaret comes to agree that she has no need for a consuming passion, for drama. It is a wholesale rejection of the portentous stuff of Challis and Morgan, and perhaps it is an attempt too to find a new

tone of voice for post-war Britain, a lower-
ing of the emotional temperature, a plea for
kindness, reflection and simple pleasure.
However, it doesn't seem as if the powers
Gibbons has used on Charles Morgan have
been very gentle. She hasn't expended much
pity on him, and the laughter is all at his
expense. In that same funeral oration,
Edith Sitwell also said: 'I am sure not one of us heard him pass a
harsh judgement, or be unkindly witty at the expense of another.'

The same could not be said of Stella Gibbons, whose wit is often
wicked and unsparing. Morgan's fiction has dated quite badly, and it
isn't full of laughs. It is difficult, though, to imagine him brutally
taking down a professional rival. It's a reminder of Gibbons's spiki-
ness, her willingness to burn bridges. She might say that a woman
had to be bolder to make herself heard above all the men, and she
would probably be right. It is sad, though, that her literary loneliness
was the almost inevitable result.

CHRIS SAUNDERS is managing director of Henry Sotheran Ltd, the oldest antiquarian bookdealer in the country, and a sporadic writer on literary subjects. He
lives in East Sussex with his wife and daughter and a house full of books. You
can hear him in Episode 12 of our podcast, 'Slightly Foxed – But Still Desirable',
discussing the world of antiquarian and second-hand bookshops.

A Farmboy Goes to War

WILLIAM PALMER

One day, and only because I asked her what life had really been like in the Blitz, my mother told me not about terrifying explosions and damage and injury, but about a cold rainy day in November 1940, when with many others she watched an endless procession of lorries and carts pass in silence through the bombed centre of Coventry. The vehicles were carrying the bodies of the dead to mass graves. Most of the memories of that time are now like this; a few words passed down through families. And, inevitably, adult witnesses of that war become fewer and fewer as the years pass.

In a way, the continuing production of war films – usually regarded with scorn by veterans of non-fictional wars – and books of popular military history is only the latest sign of a ceaseless nostalgia for the heroic; an endlessly unsatisfied need to somehow experience the feelings of those who suffered, who were there. Didn't even Samuel Johnson, a gentle man under his crust, say to Boswell, 'Every man thinks meanly of himself for not having been a soldier, or not having been to sea . . . The profession of soldiers and sailors has the dignity of danger. Mankind reverences those who have got over fear, which is so general a weakness.'

This is the direct theme of one of the first modern novels to show how war is experienced by the common soldier: *The Red Badge of Courage* by Stephen Crane. Praised to this day as one of the few realistic accounts of battle, Crane's book is set in the American Civil War

Stephen Crane, *The Red Badge of Courage* (1895)
Oxford University Press · Pb · 320pp · £7.99 · ISBN 9780199552542

of 1861–5. But Crane was not born until 1871, and the book was first published in 1895. How could such a powerfully convincing account have been written by someone with no experience of fighting?

Crane's father was a clergyman and the males on his mother's side seem to have been almost exclusively Methodist ministers. From childhood on Crane had no intention of following their example. At the age of 16, obsessed with the idea of becoming a soldier, he talked his mother into letting him transfer to a school with a military training department. He grew into an attractive, athletic boy who received a good schooling in the classics, literature, art and music – and military life.

He excelled in drill and was soon promoted to first lieutenant in the cadet corps. He read much of the vast literature that the Civil War had produced but was disappointed by many of the memoirs – 'these fellows don't tell how they felt in those scraps!' More to the point, actual vivid memories of war were provided by talk among the war veterans who helped to drill the cadets, men who had been through the fire of war in the most brutal and immediate way.

Crane did not go on to West Point; he needed immediate adventure and by the age of 19 was a professional journalist, writing for the *New York Tribune* and other papers, mostly about life among the bums and prostitutes on the Bowery, in their world of saloons, cheap hotels and brothels. He attacked police corruption and the injustice of the courts. He disguised himself as a tramp, saying that he must experience directly how such a life felt.

That is what interested Crane – how people behave, morally and physically, in extreme circumstances – how *he* himself would behave. The ultimate test was war, and the American Civil War had been devastating and bitterly fought: its causes and effects were still vividly present in the minds of ordinary Americans in Crane's youth. By writing *The Red Badge of Courage*, Crane was determined to show as closely as he could how one man would experience the horrors of war.

The cold passed reluctantly from the earth, and the retiring fogs revealed an army stretched out on the hills, resting.

So the book opens. Apart from brief flashbacks it concerns itself with just a few days of battle. Crane chose as his protagonist a young private soldier, Henry Fleming, an uneducated farm boy who has joined up in a swell of patriotism. It is in Henry's mind that we live during the battle – not in that of the young officer we see rallying and bullying his troops, who is perhaps Crane's sardonic picture of how he might himself have behaved in action.

Henry is in the Union Army camped in the hills. Across the valley and river is the camp of the Confederate Army. Henry is 18. He has joined up dreaming of valour and military glory, reflected in the admiring eyes of the girls who waved him off in his home town. He has spent months in camp, in drilling, in musketry and bayonet practice, and he has learned to accept the rough camaraderie of the other recruits.

That first morning, as the fogs disperse, they march all day, to make camp again as night falls. The next day they descend to file across the river. They make camp and sleep again. At dawn he is kicked roughly out of sleep.

> Before he was entirely awake, he found himself running down a wood road in the midst of men . . . His canteen banged rhythmically upon his thigh and his haversack bobbed softly. His musket bounced a trifle from his shoulder and made his cap feel uncertain upon his head . . . he felt carried along by a mob.

He feels excitement that 'the time had come. He was about to be measured,' and then, only a second later, terror that 'they were taking him out to slaughter'.

Locked in a mass of running men, there is no escape. He hears the first sounds of firing close at hand and the troops pass the first dead body in their path. In a clearing, they are ordered to dig in, piling mounds of earth in front of them to await the expected attack. It doesn't come. They are ordered to withdraw. The seemingly irrational orders and counter-orders irritate and bewilder them. But then they are ordered to go forward once more and to make a stand.

Through the enveloping smoke of cannon and musket, gun flashes give them their first sight of the troops rushing towards them. They fire and fire again, in seemingly endless and exhausting rounds of loading and reloading their weapons, amid smoke and shouts and screams, until the enemy suddenly retreats. Henry stands up and sees the result of the encounter on the ground.

> They lay twisted in fantastic contortions. Arms were bent and heads were turned in incredible ways. It seemed that the dead must have fallen from some great height to get into such positions. They looked to be dumped out upon the ground from the sky.

In the valley below, men still move and fight in and out of the smoke, but it seems they have won the battle.

So it was all over at last! The supreme trial had been passed. The red, formidable difficulties of war had been vanquished . . . Upon his fellows he beamed tenderness and good will . . . There were some handshakings and deep speeches with men whose features were familiar but with whom the youth now felt the bond of tied hearts.

The new bond does not last long. Before the men have had time to celebrate further, a devastating counter-attack almost sweeps their line away.

A man near him who up to this time had been working feverishly at his rifle suddenly stopped and ran with howls . . . Others began to scamper away through the smoke. The youth turned his head. He yelled then with fright and swung about . . . He began to speed toward the rear in great leaps. His rifle and cap were gone. His unbuttoned coat bulged in the wind. The flap of his cartridge box bobbed wildly, and his canteen, by its slender cord, swung out behind.

The slightly comic but earnest figure who had set out newly uniformed just a few days before has become a coward and a renegade.

The remaining two-thirds of this short book concern the shame and guilt and self-deception and deception of others in which Henry indulges to try and disguise what he has done – deserted in the face of the enemy. And more importantly it shows how he redeems himself in the eyes of others. That was what was important to Crane. He sets up the failure of a very young man and allows him a final triumph. So, although we call the book an early modern work (it had a tremendous influence on Ernest Hemingway when he came to write *A Farewell to Arms* and it changed how the great wars of the last century were dealt with in fiction), it is not a conventional 'anti-war' novel of the type that we now expect. The red badge of courage of the title is a visible wound sustained in action. The American Civil

War may have been one of the first to display the characteristics of modern warfare in its use of entrenchment and heavy artillery, but it was also a war of muskets and bayonets, and the greater part of most battles was conducted in hand-to-hand combat.

For a long time readers assumed that Crane's experience of combat came from his experiences in the Greco-Turkish and the Spanish-American wars that he covered as a correspondent. But these came some years after his book was written. He proved a seemingly fearless reporter and acted with considerable bravery when carrying, under heavy fire, supplies to wounded men in Cuba.

Stephen Crane was 23 when his novel was published. He had had a first novel privately published at his own expense and it had disappeared without trace, but *The Red Badge of Courage* was an immediate success in both America and Britain. Crane was only 28 when he died from tuberculosis in a Bavarian clinic in 1900, but his fiction, journalism and poetry fill ten volumes.

In some strange way it was as if, knowing how short a span he would have to live, Crane contrived to live his life in reverse. Tortured by doubts about his own courage, he first wrote his totally imagined novel, and then went out to seek the real dangers – courageous campaigning journalism, shipwreck and foreign wars – that would test him.

Above all, his book asks this question of every one of its readers – how would you behave in this inferno?

WILLIAM PALMER is the author of several novels. His first non-fiction work, *In Love with Hell*, a study of alcohol in the lives and works of writers, was published in 2021. You can hear him in Episode 38 of our podcast, 'Literary Drinking: Alcohol in the Lives and Work of Writers'.

Beyond the Safe Zone

RICHARD BROWN

Of all the hopeless tasks I have ever set myself, perhaps the most quixotic has been my attempt to persuade undergraduate historians to read fiction. In my experience the average student is pretty well allergic to the idea that they might ever venture beyond the safe zone of their set reading, let alone engage with something that (as they sometimes put it) 'isn't even true'. They may accept in principle the idea that fiction might in some vague and abstract sense prove personally enriching, but to suggest to a world-weary undergrad that a specific novel might have direct relevance to the actual topic they happen to be working on is to invite, nine times out of ten, a look of blank incomprehension.

A few years ago I tried, and I think entirely failed, to persuade a class of second years that because Jane Austen's *Emma* is ultimately about a failure of intelligence, a careful reading of it would improve their own understanding of decision-making in the lead-up to the Iraq War. They weren't buying it. Even my appeal to a higher authority – I had gleaned that reading of *Emma* from an essay by an impossibly august professor of international relations at Yale – could not persuade them that the story of a headstrong young woman diligently gathering and then hopelessly misanalysing intelligence might usefully illustrate certain more recent instances wherein flawed preconceptions had led to faulty conclusions.

I was not much more successful in persuading a room of im-

Italo Calvino, *Invisible Cities* (1972) · Trans. William Weaver
Vintage · Pb · 160pp · £8.99 · ISBN 9780099429838

pressionable first years that Aldous Huxley's *Brave New World* and C. S. Lewis's *That Hideous Strength* might serve them well as useful commentaries on mid-twentieth century debates about science and society. If it weren't for the fact that I actually quite like my students, and would therefore never call them such names, I might almost say that most of the time I end up casting literary pearls before swine.

Yet for all the discouragements, I persist, and the pearl that I cast most often, particularly at those wonderful, rare students who ask genuinely perceptive questions, is not *Emma* (great though it is) but something far slimmer and – I would argue – more ambitious: *Invisible Cities* (1972) by Italo Calvino. It has the most straight-forward of premises. Marco Polo is regaling his host Kublai Khan with descriptions of cities he says he has visited. These are delivered as gnomic reflections, none of which stretches over more than a couple of pages and some of which fit into a single paragraph. These accounts are framed by similarly brief glimpses of the interactions between the traveller and the emperor as they sit together and imagine distant cities. You cannot, then, get lost in the plot: in *Invisible Cities* only the cities themselves ever prove labyrinthine.

So how best to read it? It depends, I suppose, on the sort of journey you envisage for yourself. You could consume the whole thing in one breathless evening, in which case it would take on the character of a fever dream, with successive glimpses of fantastic cities settling upon one another like snow, eventually forming a layered collage of two men's thoughts. Alternatively, you could read it slowly over many weeks, mulling a passage or even a sentence at a time, in which case each chapter would become a profound prose poem of its own, an unfolding series of oracles on the nature of memory. I have read it both ways in my time, and both have their advantages. Now, though, I prefer to pass through the book like a true traveller, letting the journey itself set the pace, sometimes hurrying breathlessly onwards to the next vista, sometimes lingering to absorb fully a new or familiar sight.

One of my favourite sights in *Invisible Cities* is Octavia, the spiderweb city, suspended between two precipices with a great void yawning beneath. Octavia's inhabitants tread carefully on the narrow catwalks, and they know that the web of ropes and chains that holds their city together cannot do so forever. It is a beautiful city. It is an impossible city. It is also, in an important sense, *every* city. Here, as in so many of the places Marco Polo conjures up, the thing that is most fantastical is also the thing that is most true. It turns out that what may be fiction speaks directly to life. Apt, therefore, that the chapter on Octavia begins memorably with the line, 'If you choose to believe me, good.'

Kublai Khan is not entirely sure he *does* believe his guest. He presses him, cross-examines him, extracts the occasional concession that perhaps the real theme being explored in all these strange, beautiful accounts is not so much 'the city' as the fickle interplay of memory and imagination. In time the great Khan realizes, as we readers come to realize, that for Marco Polo all cities are ultimately Venice, his distant home. Neither he nor we can escape from our own 'first city', the place of origin that remains implicit in all our subsequent travels. Every experience we have is shaped by what we have previously known, and even our efforts to imagine something completely 'other' have to differ *from* something. Partly for this reason, another thematic undercurrent to the book is the immense difficulty, perhaps the impossibility, of true communication with another human being. In fact the dialogue between Marco Polo and Kublai Khan may not be a dialogue at all.

I worry that that last paragraph makes the poor book sound like some cute postmodern game. Perhaps it is. But maybe that's no bad thing. Games are supposed to be fun, and like good fiction they can make us feel (and therefore understand) things that the dry recitation of fact alone would otherwise struggle to depict. Though Italian, Calvino was a part of the French 'Oulipo' movement, whose members delighted in inventing elaborate structures for their work, and in so doing produced clever, playful novels that reward (but do not demand) close and thoughtful reading. Challenges and patterns abound in *Invisible Cities*, and there is a joy to be had in realizing, for example, that the names given to the cities – Clarice, Hypatia, Chloe and so on – are far from accidental, just as there is a satisfaction in pondering, long after you have closed the book, the anachronisms (radar antennae, underground trains, a munitions factory) that crop up like veiled hints throughout the text.

At any rate you do not need to be a fully paid-up fan of post-modern scholarship (I assure you I'm not) to be able to appreciate Calvino's achievement. Rather, have faith that if the prose ever veers into the realm of the obscure, it is only with good reason. (A case in point: on p.29 of my edition, we learn that 'If existence in all its moments is all of itself, Zoe is the place of indivisible existence.' It all seems very obscure – until you catch an echo of, say, T. S. Eliot's *Four Quartets*, smile to yourself, and press on to the next city.)

Memory being fickle, I don't remember when I first read *Invisible Cities*, but it must pre-date my having started keeping a diary, for in its earliest appearance there it is already marked 'R', for 'reread'. That means I was almost certainly a mere sixth-former when I first encountered it, in William Weaver's subtle, delicate translation. It may even have been one of the ways in which my past self began to imagine what it would be like to study history as a vocation. What I do know is that the next time a student asks me a good question about how – or if – we can really study the past, and I find myself stumbling through an explanation of the historian's clumsy dance between the particular and the general, I am pretty sure I know which book I will reach for. I know I risk encountering yet another blank face, but on the off chance that they take me at my word and read it, they will come across a passage that has shaped much of my thinking:

Marco Polo describes a bridge, stone by stone.

'But which is the stone that supports the bridge?' Kublai Khan asks.

'The bridge is not supported by one stone or another,' Marco answers, 'but by the line of the arch that they form.'

Kublai Khan remains silent, reflecting. Then he adds: 'Why do you speak to me of the stones? It is only the arch that matters to me.'

Polo answers: 'Without stones there is no arch.'

Here, I will tell them, is the sum of the historian's craft. Here is a deep meditation on the inter-relation of past and present, place and experience. Here is a writer grappling with what it is to discover, and the challenge of imparting that discovery to another human soul. Here, in short, is a book you really should read. If you choose to believe me, good.

RICHARD BROWN is a stay-at-home dad and occasional historian. Of all the (non-fictional) cities he has loved, his favourite is still York, where he lives with his wife and children. His article was a joint winner of the 2022 *Slightly Foxed* Writers' Competition.

J. Weston Lewis

Finding a Family

FRANCES DONNELLY

Michael Cunningham is best known for his third novel *The Hours* (1998), later made into an equally successful film. But it's his second, *A Home at the End of the World* (1991), which I consistently reread, knowing that its lyrical voice and profound insights will never fail to move me.

The story is told by four voices, two male and two female, with such tenderness and sympathy that it's clear how much the author loves his flawed characters. Bobby and Jonathan are young men growing up during the 1960s and '70s, in Cleveland, Ohio. Bobby has a conventionally happy home with an adored older brother. His life has been infused by the ordinary and the actual – meals, school, parents. But by his early teens, his life has imploded. His mother and brother are dead and his father has become an alcoholic. At Junior High, spaced out and almost feral, he meets clever, self-contained Jonathan who lives with his mother and father. They bond immediately and ferociously.

It was the kind of reckless overnight friendship particular to those who are young, lonely and ambitious. Gradually, item by item, Bobby brought over his records, his posters and his clothes to my room. He was escaping from a stale, sour smell of soiled laundry, old food and a father who moved with drunken caution from room to room.

Michael Cunningham, *A Home at the End of the World* (1991)
Penguin · Pb · 352pp · £9.99 · ISBN 9780241954539

It's not that Jonathan's family becomes Bobby's. It's that Jonathan has become Bobby's family.

The whole question of family – how it makes and mars you in almost equal measure – is one of Michael Cunningham's main concerns. But as a gay man, the questions he asks transcend the norms of the nuclear family. Who are our real family? Is it those to whom we're connected by blood? Or is it possible, through friends and lovers, to create a reconfiguration which answers our real emotional needs?

There are two female voices in the narrative, the first of whom is Alice, Jonathan's mother. Without pleasure she recalls: 'Our son brought Bobby home when they were both thirteen. He looked hungry as a stray dog and just as sly and dangerous.' But Jonathan's father Ned, who runs the local cinema, has a different take.

'That kid's in a bad way,' he remarks, after seeing Bobby ravenously demolish one of Alice's exquisite meals. 'He's a boy with no one but a father, growing up half wild. We have enough resources to give shelter to a wild boy, don't we?'

So Bobby stays and sleeps in Jonathan's room. Alice, not happy in her marriage and who's always prized her closeness to her only child, finds that that part of her life is abruptly over. She's even less happy when she discovers her son and his friend engaged in a rudimentary sexual relationship. But Bobby becomes a fixture and Alice, to her own surprise, enjoys teaching him how to cook. Jonathan leaves home for college. Bobby tries to open a restaurant, fails, then eight years later follows Jonathan to New York.

At this point in the story the final narrative voice is added: Clare, Jonathan's New York flatmate. Orange-haired, sassy, strident, a jewellery designer in her late thirties, she's 'the kind of woman always fated to play second banana in Thirties comedies'. They are, in Jonathan's words, half lovers. They share everything except a bed. Jonathan's sexual needs are taken care of by a blushing and monosyllabic bartender called Erich, referred to derisively as Dr Feelgood.

Clare has officially given up on men. But when Bobby moves into their flat she realizes there is one thing she wants that Jonathan can't give her and that is a baby. After she seduces Bobby the balance of the trio is abruptly destabilized. But eventually, uneasily, it is reconfigured. And when Clare becomes pregnant they decide the three of them will leave New York and bring up the baby together, creating the kind of family they've always yearned for.

That New York is somewhere you experience, as opposed to making it your permanent home, is wonderfully conveyed by the fact that Clare and Jonathan have furnished their flat by picking up other people's discards off the sidewalk. When they decide to leave, they simply take all their furnishings downstairs. Immediately other people appear to bear them gleefully away. You leave New York with what you brought with you: your records and your books.

But Clare has inheritance money due so they can make a proper home in an old house near Woodstock. Jonathan and Bobby successfully open the Home Café nearby. Baby Rebecca is born and adored. Finally the trio have created their own version of a family. Even Alice, widowed at 50, has begun a new life. She sets up a catering company and begins a passionate relationship with a younger man. For each of the four narrators, some kind of stability has been achieved.

Except. The time is the 1980s. This is not a novel 'about' AIDS but it offers some of the best, most truthful and most poignant writing about that terrifying time. The first, ominous note is sounded when Jonathan tells us, laconically and completely out of the blue: 'The day our friend Arthur went to hospital, I traded histories with Erich. I just want us to have an idea about the scope of each other's past. And for almost an hour we called in all our stray business, the affairs both good and bad.'

They conclude that, in terms of risk, they are somewhere towards the middle of the spectrum. 'We'd hoped vaguely to fall in love but hadn't worried because we thought we had all the time in the world. And in the meantime we'd had sex. And with each new adventure I'd imagined the prim houses and barren days of Ohio falling further away.'

At this stage AIDS is something that's happening to other people. It's only when Dr Feelgood arrives for a country weekend that a chain of events is precipitated that will determine the story's outcome. As Erich steps down from the train, Jonathan says: 'I knew as soon as I saw him.'

Can their new, fragile family absorb this information – and eventually Erich himself, as his family have disowned him?

Each time I reread this book I am reminded again of the lesson that grace, insight and kindness can be found in the most appalling circumstances. Perhaps Bobby, privately, sums it up best: 'There is a beauty in the world, though it's harsher than we ever expect it to be.'

FRANCES DONNELLY still lives in the Waveney valley in Suffolk and is profoundly grateful for her Covid vaccinations. She never got a rescue dog.

At Sea with Slocum

JOHN KEAY

Books can be ill served by the company they keep. In my childhood home they were shelved in the only bookcase and consisted entirely of anthologies published as Reader's Digest Condensed Books plus the several volumes of Churchill's *The Second World War*. None was ever read or even consulted. They were just part of the furniture. Something as slight as Joshua Slocum's *Sailing Alone around the World* was lost amongst them. 'That was Dad's favourite book,' said my mother as we cleared the house after his death. I'd no idea he had a favourite book, and it was not till some years later that, hoping to understand him better, I began turning its pages.

It was New England, 1892. The canvas-covered hulk was still just about recognizable as a sailboat, albeit one that had seen better days. 'Affectionately propped up in a field some distance from salt water', she had last worked on the oyster beds of the Acushnet estuary but by 1892 had been sitting there, high and dry in her Massachusetts meadow outside Fairhaven, for seven years. A tow to the breaker's yard in nearby New Bedford looked overdue. It was either that or rot.

'She wants some repairs,' ventured the whaling captain who was disposing of her; her prospective buyer suspected the whaler of 'having', as he put it, 'something of a joke on me'. But himself a shipwright and the skipper of numerous sailing vessels in an age that preferred

---

I have used the version of *Sailing Alone around the World* included in the anniversary edition of *The Voyages of Joshua Slocum*, edited by Walter Magnes Teller (Sheridan House, New York, 1995). There are many other editions available, but few contain his other works and sundry correspondence.

steam, the buyer badly needed a command. Terms were agreed, proprietorship of the 'very antiquated sloop called the *Spray*' passed from Captain Eben Pierce to Captain Joshua Slocum, and with axe in hand a spry but balding Slocum bounded off into the woods, there to fell an oak for a new keel, cut timbers for a complete rebuild and so make ready for the voyage of the century.

Where others spied a hulk, Slocum already saw a kindred spirit. The *Spray* would become the pride and joy of his later years, his faithful adjunct, his muse and literary device. More surprisingly, where others discerned just a boat, the captain envisioned a book. To a man of enquiring mind who could claim only two years of schooling, books had become as enticing as foreign lands. There was even a local precedent. Fifty years earlier the young Herman Melville had set sail from New Bedford as a deckhand on a whaler called the *Acushnet*. The voyage took Melville round the Horn into the South Pacific, providing inspiration for *Typhoon* and material for *Moby-Dick*. Slocum knew them both. He would even duplicate part of Melville's itinerary before crossing the Pacific to complete what he called his 'voyage round', the first ever solo circumnavigation. But while Melville's 360-ton *Acushnet* had been 100 feet long with two decks, three masts and a crew of twenty, the *Spray* was shaping up as a sloop of under 37 feet with a single mast, a net weight of 9 tons and a crew of one – Slocum himself.

As well as noting Melville's itinerary, Slocum had toyed with Melville's career path. In the 1880s he had self-published his account of a calamitous voyage to Montevideo in command of a Baltimore-built clipper. The ship was the *Aquidneck* but the book appeared as *The Voyage of the 'Liberdade'*, that being the name Slocum had given to a houseboat ('half Cape Ann dory, half Japanese sampan') which he and his family had constructed and then sailed home when the *Aquidneck* was wrecked off the South American coast. 'This literary craft of mine', began his account of that Swiss Family Robinson adventure, 'goes out laden with the facts of the strange happenings on a home afloat.' The words could have served as the preface to its more famous sequel, *Sailing Alone around the World*. Slocum already likened a blank page to the open ocean and his tender narrative to a craft in which to cross it.

Throughout 1893 Slocum laboured with maul and adze above the Fairhaven shoreline. Cash being in short supply, he was obliged to take odd jobs including piloting an iron barge described as a 'gun boat fitted with torpedo tubes'. This contraption, the antithesis of all a sail-loving mariner held most dear, had to be towed from New York to Bahia for delivery to the Brazilian navy, Slocum acting as 'navigator in command'. It was an implausible assignment and prompted only the brief account which was penned of an evening in the *Spray*'s newly built cabin as the author rested from another day's 'sailorizing' – now mostly planking and caulking.

By 1894 the *Spray* was ready to return to her element. Nothing is recorded of the launch except that 'she sat on the water like a swan'. Her master was rightly proud of her. 'Put together as strongly as wood and iron could make her', she yet 'flew' when Captain Pierce came for a trial sail. The rest of the year was spent fishing north to Boston and, by way of a farewell, cruising up the coast to Slocum's Nova Scotia birthplace. Meanwhile he bombarded New York's publishers. 'My mind is deffinately fixed on one thing and that is to go round –' he told the man acting as his agent, 'to go with care and judgement and speak of what I see.' Others could correct his spelling. What Slocum wanted was a serialization deal with a major journal, plus an advance. Both eventually materialized.

At the port of Gloucester he took on potatoes, coffee and dried cod but for reading material he relied on his publishing contacts. His later editor records the titles that arrived in one of several boxloads: Darwin's *The Descent of Man* and *The Expression of Emotions in Man and Animals*, Macaulay's *History of England* and Trevelyan's *Life of Macaulay*, Irving's *Life of Columbus*, Boswell's *Life of Samuel Johnson*, Cervantes' *Don Quixote*, Twain's *Life on the Mississippi*, 'one or more titles by Robert Louis Stevenson', a set of Shakespeare, and in 'the poet's corner', as he called it, works of Lamb, Moore, Burns, Tennyson and Longfellow. The *Spray's* library outweighed the potatoes. If nothing else, the captain, should he return, would be uncommonly well read.

By 24 April 1895 he was ready. At noon the *Spray* weighed anchor and was waved off from the Boston waterfront.

A thrilling pulse beat high in me. My step was light on deck in the crisp air. I felt there could be no turning back, and that I was engaging in an adventure the meaning of which I thoroughly understood. I had taken little advice from anyone, for I had a right to my own opinions in matters pertaining to the sea.

The confidence was born of his forty years before the mast, many of them spent boatbuilding in the Philippines and ferrying exotic cargoes in the Far East. By one calculation Slocum had already been round the world five times. His knowledge of oceanography was extensive and his ability to read the winds and currents probably unsurpassed. He disdained instrumentation. For a chronometer he had a tin clock, which soon lost its minute-hand and required an occasional 'boiling'. A lead was used to measure depths and a towed log to measure distances travelled. Bearings depended on a compass and meridian observations. At night he hung a lantern from the masthead and, below deck, lit a two-burner lamp for reading by. 'By some small contriving', the lamp also served as a stove.

The *Spray* was excelling herself. Despite fog and storms, she covered the first 1,200 miles in ten days. Her captain's 'acute pain of solitude' eased when the Azores yielded fresh fruit, only to be succeeded by greater pain from accompanying plums with goat's cheese.

For two days Slocum lay groaning on the cabin floor. He must have been reading Washington Irving's *Columbus*, for it was one of Columbus's pilots who materialized at the *Spray's* helm and sailed her through the impending gale. The hallucination vanished as he recovered. 'To my astonishment the *Spray* was still heading as I had left her. Columbus himself could not have held her more exactly on course.' He ditched the plums and headed for Gibraltar.

The plan was to continue east through the Mediterranean and the Suez Canal but the ill repute of the Barbary pirates prompted an about-turn. Pursued by a rakish felucca, he scuttled back into the Atlantic and made for Brazil. September brought sightings of the Canary and Cape Verde islands. The *Spray* was making the most of the trade winds. An over-friendly turtle improved his diet; flying fish obligingly flopped on deck, one slithering down the hatch straight into the pan. On 5 October anchor was cast in Pernambuco harbour; 'forty days from Gibraltar, and all well on board . . . I was never in better trim . . . and eager for the more perilous experience of rounding the Horn.'

The Horn obliged. Instead of rounding the Cape, he tackled the Magellan Strait between the mainland and Tierra del Fuego – twice in fact. Battling repeated storms through a maze of islands, the *Spray* entered the Pacific only to be driven south towards what he supposed were the Falkland Islands. It was actually more of Tierra del Fuego. He turned north again and repeated his passage through the strait. Marauding Fuegians were kept at bay by strewing the deck with carpet tacks. On stepping aboard, the raiders 'howled like a pack of hounds. I had hardly use for a gun.'

Two months after first braving the strait, and a year after leaving Boston, he was again alone in open water. The Pacific would be crossed by island-hopping in what reads like a literary pilgrimage. A first landfall was made on Juan Fernandez where Alexander Selkirk, the inspiration for Defoe's *Robinson Crusoe*, had been marooned in the early 1700s. The island now had a population of forty-five.

Slocum regaled them with coffee and doughnuts from the *Spray*'s galley and visited the castaway's cave. He so liked the island he couldn't understand why Selkirk ever left it.

After a seventy-two-day crossing – 'a long time to be at sea alone' – it was a similar story in Samoa. Stevenson had died at Vailima, his island home, just as Slocum was completing the rebuild of the *Spray* in Fairhaven. But Fanny, the author's American wife, was still there, as were her son and daughter-in-law. All three piled into the *Spray*'s green dinghy (actually a customized dory in which Slocum did his washing) while Fanny sang 'The Owl and the Pussy-cat'. As valedictory she presented the *Spray* with new spars and the captain with 'a great directory of the Indian Ocean' belonging to her husband.

Australia marked the halfway point. Slocum knew it well; it was where he had met his first wife. The rest of 1896 was spent in Australian waters as was much of 1897. Unlike later solo circumnavigators he was in no hurry. He was fêted in Sydney and Melbourne, explored Tasmania, was nearly wrecked on the Great Barrier Reef and hit on a new source of income: visitors were charged for a tour of the *Spray* and public engagements were welcomed. Having read his way round half the world he would lecture his way round the other half.

In *Sailing Alone* the homeward voyage runs to just forty pages. In actuality it took nearly a year with landfalls and lectures in the Cocos islands, Mauritius, Durban and Cape Town (where he failed to impress the explorer H. M. Stanley). The voyage was not without alarms; 'but it was to me like reading a book and more interesting as I turned the pages over'.

Published in 1900, *Sailing Alone* proved an instant success and has seldom been out of print. Nine years later the *Spray* and her master disappeared off the Massachusetts coast and were never seen again.

JOHN KEAY's *Himalaya: Exploring the Roof of the World* was published by Bloomsbury in 2022. He has never owned a boat, but his father was a master mariner.

Against the Current

Wallace Stegner seems on the brink of being forgotten. Half a century ago he was acknowledged as a major figure in American letters; one of his novels won the Pulitzer Prize, and another the National Book Award. He was highly regarded, not just as a novelist, but also as a pioneering teacher of creative writing and as a mentor to a generation of younger writers. Yet when I asked around recently, not one of my bookish acquaintances recognized his name. I had never heard of him myself until a friend recommended him on a pandemic-relieving country walk.

Even in his native land Stegner is now neglected. In 2020 he was the subject of the first of a series of *New York Times* pieces on overlooked or under-read American writers by the critic A. O. Scott. 'Stegner's books abide in an under-visited stretch of the American canon,' wrote Scott, 'like a national park you might drive past on the way to a theme park or a ski resort.' It was an apt simile, because the American landscape in all its variety and majesty permeates Stegner's fiction.

My walking friend kindly sent me a copy of Stegner's *Crossing to Safety* (1987). I was slow to pick it up but when I did finally read it, I found it profoundly satisfying. It is one of those books that reminds you of the solace to be found in reading. Since finishing it I have been praising it to anyone who will listen, and I know of at least half a dozen people who have read and enjoyed it on my recommenda-

Wallace Stegner, *Crossing to Safety* (1987)
Penguin · Pb · 352pp · £9.99 · ISBN 9780141394954

tion. Now I have the opportunity to proselytize to readers of *Slightly Foxed.*

Crossing to Safety is the story of two couples, the Langs and the Morgans, who meet at a Midwestern university in the late 1930s and who are immediately drawn to each other: so much so that they form a lasting bond. Both couples are then newly married and full of plans for the future. Both husbands are English teachers, ambitious for the tenure which will guarantee their future careers; both wives are pregnant, beginning a different type of adventure, one both dramatic and humdrum. One couple has money, the other does not. One man gets tenure, one does not. One becomes a successful novelist, the other a less successful poet. Their circumstances diverge, yet they remain close, through all the frictions, the jealousies, the disappointments, the necessary compromises, the corrosion of ideals and the ageing process itself. The novel is a meditation on friendship, and on marriage, and the way in which life turns out.

When they meet for the first time in Madison, Wisconsin, the circumstances of the two couples could scarcely be more different. Larry Morgan, who comes from Arizona, personifies the energy and self-reliance of the American West. Orphaned as a teenager, Larry has nothing but what he can earn, and struggles to make enough to support his wife Sally, the daughter of impoverished Greek immigrants, and their growing family. He is determined to get on, and he is proud of his achievements as a writer. Sid Lang, the son of a wealthy Pittsburgh industrialist, is more ambivalent and less assertive; he wants to be a poet, but something holds him back. (Towards the end of the novel there is an excruciating moment when Larry, searching for Sid, discovers a rhyming dictionary, concealed spine inwards, on Sid's study bookshelf.)

Sid allows himself to be ruled and indeed emasculated by his forceful and exuberant wife Charity, who comes from a long line of wealthy New Englanders, accustomed for generations to the benefits of privilege. She is both generous and domineering. There is love between all four of them, but there is also a tension between Larry and Charity throughout. He disapproves of her treatment of Sid; she remains defiant. Even while she is dying of cancer, she is still giving the orders. Meanwhile Sally, who has been crippled by polio, is calm and resigned.

Crossing to Safety was Stegner's last novel, published when he was nearly eighty. The book is narrated by Larry in old age, looking back over the events of half a lifetime, a perspective which gives the novel a nostalgic, elegiac quality.

> What ever happened to the passion we all had to improve our-selves, live up to our potential, leave a mark on the world? . . .
> Instead the world has left marks on us. We got older. Life chas-tened us so that now we lie waiting to die, or walk on canes, or sit on porches where once the young juices flowed strongly, and feel old and inept and confused.

Larry wakes early one August morning in a Vermont cottage, part of the compound where they have holidayed with the Langs for decades; he strolls out alone, leaving his wife sleeping, and climbs up the shoulder of a hill as the sun rises, and pauses to gaze down

> at the sleeping unchanged village, the lake like a pool of mer-cury, the varying greens of mayfields and meadows and sugar-brush and black spruce woods, all of it lifting and warming as the stretched shadows shorten.
>
> There it was, there it is, the place where during the best time of our lives friendship had its home and happiness its head-quarters.

Battell Pond, where Charity's family have their summer retreat, is an arcadia in the American tradition of the simple life: another Walden, where living close to nature nourishes the spirit. Stegner, a committed environmentalist, shares this pastoral ideal; yet he is too sharp an observer not to notice that this rural retreat is as artificial in its own way as the parkland of eighteenth-century England. The only moments when you will see a crowd at this discreet summer colony, he remarks, is at 'summer auctions, and at the village store at the hour when the *New York Times* is delivered'.

Not much happens in *Crossing to Safety*. The couples remain married, and no one has an affair. The most dramatic moment occurs during a hike through the woods, when Sally becomes ill, and has to be carried out of the wilderness. Stegner had a distaste for the casual promiscuity and the 'wife-swapping' (how dated that term, once so fashionable, now seems!) that featured so prominently in the work of a novelist with whom he was sometimes unfavourably compared, John Updike.

Yet despite this lack of action, *Crossing to Safety* is compelling. In Stegner's hands, marriage itself acquires an epic, enduring quality. Larry accepts the inexorable passage of time and its concomitants, mortality and loss, but he also clings to his memories, and to the value of long-lasting love.

> We weren't indifferent. We lived in our times, which were hard times. We had our interests, which were mainly literary and intellectual and only occasionally, inescapably, political. But what memory brings back from there is not politics, or the meagerness of living on $150 a month, or even the writing I was doing, but the details of friendship – parties, picnics, walks, midnight conversations, glimpses from the occasional unencumbered hours. *Amicitia* lasts better than *res publica*, and at least as well as *ars poetica*.

Stegner is hard to categorize. In some passages he seems like a left-leaning critic of capitalism, with all its crassness and waste. In others he appears deeply conservative. What concerns him most are those values he wants to protect: the environment, family, community. He proudly declared himself 'a square'; he stood firm against the current of his times. Perhaps this stubborn resistance to modish preoccupations explains why he is less often read these days. In a collection of essays published in 1996 and entitled *Why I Can't Read Wallace Stegner*, the Native American critic Elizabeth Cook-Lynn deplored the absence of minorities in his work. She had a point; yet twenty-five years on 'cultural appropriation' is being deplored. So perhaps Stegner was not so square after all.

One aspect of *Crossing to Safety* that fascinated me was how distinctly American the book is. My late wife Robyn was American, and I recognized in the novel dozens of details that I had learned from her and her family, who themselves had been academics in the Midwest. She and I once stayed in a rather uncomfortable Vermont cabin, kept by educated New Yorkers as a refuge from the city. I don't think that Robyn ever read the book, and it saddens me to reflect that she never will.

Another reason why the book appealed to me may be that I have reached what one might call the philosophical stage of life: on the cusp between middle age and old age, a period when one spends as much time looking back as looking forward. Many of the hopes I once cherished have faded or disappeared altogether, but I have learned to value more that which remains. This, I think, is the meaning of the novel's somewhat cryptic and otherwise rather forgettable title, taken from a poem by Robert Frost:

> I could give all to Time except – except
> What I myself have held. But why declare
> The things forbidden that while the Customs slept
> I have crossed to Safety with? For I am There,
> And what I would not part with I have kept.

ADAM SISMAN's most recent book is *The Professor and the Parson: A Story of Desire, Deceit and Defrocking* (2019). You can hear him in Episode 6 of our podcast, 'Well-Written Lives', discussing the art of biography.

Verse and Worse

ALASTAIR GLEGG

If the name Baring-Gould seems vaguely familiar, perhaps you grew up as I did, exposed every Sunday to *Hymns Ancient and Modern*. The Reverend Sabine Baring-Gould (1834–1924) wrote many of them, including such traditional favourites as 'Onward, Christian Soldiers' and 'Now the Day is Over'. He was a hagiographer and an extraordinarily prolific writer, credited with over 1,240 publications on various subjects. He also found the time to father fourteen children, one of whom emigrated to America where his grandson, William Baring-Gould, was born in Minnesota in 1913.

William certainly took after his grandfather when it came to research and is best known for his biography of Sherlock Holmes, a major scholarly undertaking which plausibly fits together all the famous cases and stories, and convincingly fills in the gaps. I think, however, that you really need to be a member of the Baker Street Irregulars to fully appreciate all the allusions and connections.

William and his wife Ceil (Lucile) produced *The Annotated Mother Goose* in 1962. It might perhaps be described as a coffee-table book, but it is not one of those extravagantly illustrated travelogues or a volume packed with photographs of impossibly perfect gardens. It is a book unlike any other that I have enjoyed and one from which I have learned a lot; also one in which the footnotes and illustrations are more compelling than the rhymes they describe. It includes nearly

William S. and Ceil Baring-Gould, *The Annotated Mother Goose* (1962) and William S. Baring-Gould, *The Lure of the Limerick* (1967), are out of print but we can obtain second-hand copies.

a thousand verses, although some of them are variations on a theme and others might more properly be termed folk songs, and nearly a thousand footnotes. This may sound daunting and even boring, so here is an early example to confute that impression: in England (the origin of most of them) the verses are generally called nursery rhymes, often associated with Old Mother Goose as a teller of tales. Who she was is a mystery: there are various theories going back hundreds of years, 'But now it is time for the New World to put in its claim,' writes William: Elizabeth Foster was born in Charleston, South Carolina, in 1665. At the age of 27 she married Isaac Goose who was then 55 and had been married before, and so she became stepmother to his ten children. She herself bore Isaac six more – perhaps she might also be the original Old Woman Who Lived in a Shoe – and she was grandmother and teller of tales to dozens of others. 'True or not, it is a pleasant story, and it would be cheering to Americans to think that "Mother Goose", like Sherlock Holmes, may have been American.' William's tongue was often firmly in his cheek, and (to mix metaphors) he must have enjoyed pulling the legs of his numerous English cousins.

Many of the rhymes have a long history, and some were printed on handbills. The first surviving collection, *Mother Goose's Melodies*, was published in Boston in 1719, and *Tom Thumb's Pretty Song Book (Volume II)* 'for the diversion of all Little Masters and Mistresses' came out in London in 1744. Only one copy is known to exist, a treasured possession of the British Library.

They cover every imaginable theme: lullabies and counting songs, prayers and memory aids, riddles and tongue-twisters, games and charms, proverbs and weather lore, and many that are simply entertaining nonsense. Some certainly had political and religious undertones, but as William dryly points out, 'some students may, perhaps, have been a little overzealous in reading meaning into rhymes where no meaning was ever intended'. There can, of course, be no definitive answer: 'Mary, Mary [or 'Mistress Mary'] Quite

Contrary' is generally thought to refer to Mary, Queen of Scots, but is an example of how interpretations can differ. William cites the theory that the 'pretty maids all in a row' may have been 'the Four Marys', her ladies-in-waiting, and the cockleshells may have been decorations on a dress given to her by the Dauphin. As a child I was told that the pretty maids were nuns (Mary was after all a Roman Catholic), and that the cockleshells were a reference to those carried by the Palmers, so called because they brought back palm-leaf crosses from their pilgrimages to the Holy Land. Who knows? And does it really matter to children?

There are of course slightly different versions of many of the rhymes, not just between Britain and America, but within Britain itself, and quite naturally we all tend to think that the versions we learned as children are the 'proper' ones. William notes the variations, and often explains them: there are all sorts of fascinating scraps of information and folklore throughout the collection. For instance, I remember the rhyme 'Taffy was a Welshman' (perhaps now considered politically incorrect) but was unaware of the origin of the name: 'The Welsh pronunciation of the name "Davy", David, became a nickname given the Welshman by the Englishman.' The name 'Margery' (as in 'Seesaw, Margery Daw') was apparently used mostly by poor country people, and a Daw was 'an untidy woman, slut, slattern' (*Oxford English Dictionary*). 'The suspicion arises that Margery Daw, whoever she may have been, was no better than she should be.'

The volume is beautifully and profusely illustrated, the early sections with old woodcuts and engravings, the later ones with a wealth of wonderful drawings by well-known artists, some of whom produced their own collections of nursery rhymes, such as Arthur Rackham, Kate Greenaway and Randolph

Arthur Rackham

Randolph Caldecott

Caldecott. Their styles are very different: Rackham's delightful nursery rhyme illustrations are generally (and sensibly) much simpler than those he produced for other subjects such as Grimm's tales and the German legends; Kate Greenaway's children are models of good behaviour and decorum; Randolph Caldecott obviously took a sly delight in country scenes and bucolic characters.

William cites more than 130 books containing or about nursery rhymes – half of them written before 1900 – but that is as much a measure of their importance in social history as it is a sign of nostalgia for simpler childhood days and the curiosity inevitably aroused by some of the verses. Who was Old King Cole? Bobby Shafto? The fine lady upon a white horse? Where was Tom Tiddler's Ground? Why is the little red beetle called a ladybird? Which rhyme is quoted in *King Lear*? The answers are all in his fascinating collection.

William published another entertaining volume of verses, but this is one you might want to remove from the coffee table when Great-Aunt Gladys is visiting you. *The Lure of the Limerick: An Uninhibited History* was first published in 1967 and contains nearly 500 examples, with appropriate illustrations by the French Art Deco artist André Domin, Oscar Wilde's young associate Aubrey Beardsley and – by way of contrast – Edward Lear. William realized that some people might be surprised:

> Why, it may be asked, should anyone *want* to write about such an indecorous form of verse as the limerick? . . . Hardly an educated man is now alive who does not treasure in his memory at least one limerick, proper or improper. The chances are that he did not read it in a book or a magazine: it was passed on to him by word of mouth, by 'oral tradition'. As such, the limerick is authentic folklore – a vital part of our heritage.

There are of course perfectly proper limericks about scientific phenomena:

> There was a young lady named Bright
> Whose speed was far faster than light;
> She went out one day,
> In a relative way,
> And returned on the previous night.

Then there are others such as the one that Monsignor Ronald Knox persuaded an unwary newspaper editor to run as a classified advertisement:

> Evangelical vicar, in want, of a portable second-hand font, would dispose of the same, for a portrait, in frame, of the Bishop-Elect of Vermont,

and W. S. Gilbert's sarcastic response to the simplicity of Edward Lear's verses:

> There was an old man of St Bees,
> Who was stung on the arm by a wasp.
> When asked, 'Does it hurt?'
> He replied, 'No, it doesn't;
> I'm so glad it wasn't a hornet.'

Edward Lear

The origin of the limerick is obscure, but some scholars claim to be able to trace it back to the fifteenth century, and there are several examples in Shakespeare's plays of very similar verse forms. Even some nursery rhymes follow the format – 'Hickory, Dickory, Dock', for instance – but the Founding Father of the limerick, in William's opinion, was Edward Lear with his *Book of Nonsense* (1846), although with few exceptions Lear 'ignored the whiplash ending which makes the modern limerick so effective' and often repeated the end of the first line:

There was an old man of Thermopylae,
Who never did anything properly:
But they said, 'If you choose
To boil eggs in your shoes,
You shall never remain in Thermopylae.'

William traces the development and origins of the limerick, and provides examples of many famous authors from Lewis Carroll to Robert Louis Stevenson who ventured into this creative realm, including W. H. Auden:

The Marquis de Sade and Genet
Are most highly thought of today,
But torture and treachery
Are not my sort of lechery,
So I've given my copies away.

Auden was on the right track however because, generally speaking,

The limerick packs laughs anatomical
Into space that is quite economical.
But the good ones I've seen
So seldom are clean
And the clean ones so seldom are comical.

The second half of this unusual book consists of a colourful collection of mostly bawdy limericks, many of them, as might be expected, recording the escapades of young men and women anywhere from Algiers to Zion:

There was a young girl of La Plata
Who was widely renowned as a farta.
Her deafening reports
At the Argentine sports
Made her much in demand as a starta.

She probably did not have much in common with Little Bo Peep, although both are attributed to the same prolific author, 'Anon.'

William Baring-Gould died of a stroke in 1967 at the age of 54. He left an extraordinary legacy: mischievously entertaining accounts of meticulous literary research into subjects no serious academic would dare to explore – a fictional detective, children's rhymes and questionable limericks. I wonder what he would have tackled next.

ALASTAIR GLEGG lives on Vancouver Island and has not composed any nursery rhymes. He was, however, delighted to hear that one of his own limericks had been passed on in the men's room at Swan's Hotel.

André Domin

Reading between the Lines

MAGGIE FERGUSSON

'The trouble with prison', a former probation officer once told me, 'is that nobody wants to be there': not the prisoners, obviously, nor the staff. If that's true, it would mean that in HMP Wandsworth, a squat black fortress that was the site of 135 executions between 1878 and 1961, there are more than 2,000 people – roughly 1,600 prisoners and 600 staff – yearning to be somewhere else.

Walk down one of the corridors radiating from the central hall, and you can see why. Your senses are assaulted. The noise is relentless: banging on cell doors, clanging of iron gates, shouting. The air feels as if it has stood still for years: you long to install an industrial fan to whip it up. There's a smell of old food, and worse. And there's almost no natural light. Victims of 'prison pallor', the men drift about like shoals of ghosts. It would be easy to lose track of the time of day, and even the time of year – except that, in summer, the cells heat up like ovens. Designed for single occupants, most are now shared by two men. If you lay on one of the bunks and reached out, you'd touch the opposite wall before your arm was straight. The thought of being banged up with a cellmate you don't like, or even trust, is terrifying.

And yet I love my monthly visits to 'Wanno'. The hour and a half I spend with a group of about ten men is challenging, thought-provoking and often entertaining. There's sadness, but always laughter too. As I leave to catch the bus home, and the men are locked back into their cells, I hope we all have much to mull over.

The charity was set up in 1999. For more details visit www.prisonreadinggroups. org.uk.

It was in the 1990s that Sarah Turvey and Jenny Hartley, academics at the University of Roehampton, decided to do some research into reading groups – then becoming all the rage amongst middle-class women. The benefits of these groups were not just literary and intellectual, they found, but psychological: they built communities, eased loneliness. If this is what they could offer the middle classes, Sarah and Jenny wondered, how much more might they benefit offenders, male and female, serving lengthy sentences in prisons up and down the UK?

'Getting into prisons is much harder than getting out of them,' says Sarah. Today, there are forty-eight reading groups, but when the charity began, over twenty years ago, there were just two: one in HMP Coldingley in Surrey and one in HMP Bullingdon in Bicester. Sarah was insistent on just two things: first, that the groups must be purely voluntary; there should be no whiff of formal, compulsory education, and no certificates or tests; no right or wrong. If a prisoner chooses to say that he'd rather 'eat my eyeballs than reread *On Chesil Beach*', that's fine. Second, it should be the prisoners who choose the books they want to read – albeit helped by suggestions from the volunteer working with them. Once a book is chosen, a copy is given to each member of the group. They have a month to read it before reconvening for discussion. It is a simple, effective formula.

The most successful books allow the prisoners to vent their feelings. When we read *Animal Farm*, I asked my group what they thought was the best kind of political system – was democracy in this country working, for example? Absolutely not, they agreed. 'We need to get rid of all Etonians,' one growled. 'We need the people in charge to have been to state schools, and grown up on estates, so they can understand where we're coming from.'

I never suggest a book with the aim of prising open prisoners' pasts, but I'm struck by how often that's what happens. In the first session I oversaw, some years back, the men had been reading *Toast*, the memoir in which Nigel Slater looks back on his childhood through the prism of 1960s food – Arctic roll, grilled grapefruit, Nesquik. One man volunteered that his parents had taught him to cook as a child, putting a chair back-to-front against the stove so he could stir Bolognese sauce without getting burned (such a touching image: what on earth went wrong?). He was frightened that by the time he was released from prison, he'd have forgotten how to cook.

'I'm sure you won't,' I reassured him. 'Cooking's like riding a bike: you don't forget how to do it.'

'But I've got thirteen years.'

Another man told us he'd been born in HMP Holloway, where his mother was an inmate. She'd died when he was small, and – like so many prisoners – he'd grown up in foster care. His 'father' was an abusive monster, but his mother tried to make things right, laying snack-packs of Jaffa Cakes on his pillow at night. By the time the group next met, he had moved on. I often wonder what's become of him.

I suppose I should have guessed that *Stuart: A Life Backwards*, Alexander Masters's extraordinary biography of homeless some-time-jailbird Stuart Shorter, would inspire strong reactions. 'Stuart's just like me,' one man said, 'mistake after mistake after mistake.' Stuart's description of being visited in prison – the anticipation before, the loneliness after – had struck a chord with him. Visits from his family, this man said, had become so painful – his brother con-stantly complaining about the cost of catching a train to see him – that he'd asked them never to visit him again.

'When was that?'

'2007.'

But memories stirred up by books can be joyous as well as heart-breaking. For our first meeting post-lockdown the group had read *The Old Man and the Sea*, and it turned out, to my astonishment, that in his life before prison a member of the group had been a mar-lin fisherman and was able to describe for us the beauty of the creature, with its long, shining snout. One man wondered whether, when Hemingway writes of the sharks attacking the marlin's carcass, it was really a metaphor for how literary critics had stripped him bare. Not for the first time, I realized that many of the men I meet in Wandsworth are a great deal cleverer than I am.

Generally, we end with a poem – though I find it impossible to gauge what the men will like. When I took in one of my favourite poems by George Mackay Brown, they unanimously agreed that it was 'rubbish'. But when I introduced them to Walter de la Mare's 'The Listeners', expecting them to find it impossibly old-fashioned, they loved it, passing it round the group and reading a verse each at a quick canter.

'Was Walter de la Mare a Christian?' one asked.

'I don't know. Why?'

'Well, these lines, "Tell them I came, and no one answered/That I kept my word, he said", they sound like Jesus, don't they?'

Not all men feel able to share their thoughts like this – at least not to begin with. But, given time, most of those who begin by sitting on the edge of the group, arms crossed and silent, gradually begin to open up. 'Can we read *My Family and Other Animals*?' asked one man at the end of a session during which he had said not a word. So we did – transporting ourselves one dark, wet, winter afternoon from dismal Wandsworth to sun-soaked Corfu.

'Don't you feel scared?' some of my friends ask. The answer is, 'No. Never.' I know 'my' men are serving long sentences, but, as I've no idea what they've actually done, I'm far more likely to feel frustrated than afraid. Sometimes, the room we are meant to meet in has been double-booked, and we have to sit in the passageway where it's almost impossible to hear yourself think. More than once, I've received a text as I'm making my way to Wandsworth on the bus: a prisoner has gone missing and the whole place is in lockdown. The reading group has been cancelled. Or a prisoner will apologize and say that he hasn't been able to read the book because he's *still* waiting for new glasses. And then there's 'churn': it's not unusual to arrive and find that half the prisoners from the previous session have been moved on.

In the face of all this, I never cease to be amazed by the dedication of the wonderful prison librarian. He not only oversees our groups but also organizes 'Storybook Dads' weekends, when prisoners' children are welcomed in to have their dads read to them. And he makes sure, for those new to the prison, that there is a 'Books for first-nighters' trolley, with fiction and non-fiction carefully chosen to ease anguish. Despite what my probation officer friend says, here is a rare example of somebody who really does want to be in prison: being a prison librarian is not just a job but a vocation. Recently, he took me to look around his library. It is a light, orderly, comfortable space, with books to suit every taste and reading ability. I was impressed. He smiled: 'I try to make it a little piece of paradise.'

MAGGIE FERGUSSON has volunteered with Prison Reading Groups for the past four years.

Bibliography

Coming attractions

YSENDA MAXTONE GRAHAM lifts up her voice · ROBIN BLAKE snoops about with Simenon · RACHEL COOKE enjoys a French lesson · SAMUEL SALOWAY-COOKE feels somewhat flat · DAISY HAY delights in *Emma* · WILLIAM PALMER goes down the pub with Myles · URSULA BUCHAN remembers *A Day in Summer* · CHRISTOPHER RUSH has a nasty moment on Dartmoor · SAM LEITH does his best to grow up

DISCOVER FASCINATING HISTORY

History Today magazine digs that bit deeper, exploring the people and events that shaped our world with erudite and thought-provoking writing from today's leading experts. Whether you are a seasoned history buff, or simply want a better understanding of life past and present, *History Today* is guaranteed to inform and entertain.

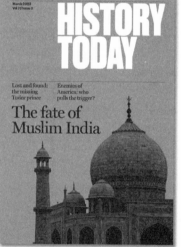